GHOST SCRIBBLER

Searching for Reagan, Brando and the King of Pop

A MEMOIR BY ROBERT LINDSEY

Books by Robert Lindsey

The Falcon and the Snowman

The Flight of the Falcon

A Gathering of Saints

Irresistible Impulse

Ronald Reagan: An American Life*

Brando: Songs My Mother Taught Me**

*In collaboration with Ronald Reagan

**In collaboration with Marlon Brando

With Love

To Susan, Steve,

Erin, Ryan, Adrian and Jessie

And, of course, to Sandy,

Still my Staff of Life

PART ONE

1

My wife and I were hosting six friends for dinner when Marlon Brando called on a Saturday night. It wasn't unusual. He often called to chat, sometimes long past midnight. When I told him I was having a dinner party and promised to call him back later, Marlon began to cry. At first I couldn't make out what he was trying to say, then I did:

Someone he knew-- *someone very famous, a thirty-five-year- old man-* -had just left his home after admitting that he had *married* an eleven - year-old boy earlier that day and given him a wedding ring.

Marlon said he didn't know what to do.

'What would you do?," he said, sobbing so hard he was choking. "He said he's *in love* with the boy."

I'll return to this telephone call after awhile--what came before, what came later--after looking back on the journey that led to it.

Near the corner of Century Boulevard and Prairie Avenue across from the Hollywood Park racetrack in Inglewood, California, there were for many years two bleak and sad trailer camps. I spent much of my youth living alternately in one or the other, depending how cheaply my mother could negotiate the rent for the concrete slab that was home to our seventeen foot house trailer and an adjacent nook covered by a tin awning that sheltered my bed from the rain. Toilets and a shower were in a grey cinder block building thirty yards away.

My first dreams of becoming a reporter took root when I was lying in this bed, probably during fourth or fifth grade while I was home sick from school listening to a radio soap opera about a newspaperman called "Front Page Farrell." In fifth grade, I started my parochial school's first student newspaper. After my sixth grade teacher, Sister Anne Louise, graded one of my compositions with a red-penciled "A" and said maybe I should think about becoming a writer, I was hooked.

I was born, I'm told, January 4, 1935 in Glendale, California, which, like Inglewood, was a Depression-battered suburb of Los Angeles. My parents were married then.

My mother, Claire Elizabeth Schulz, was born in Detroit in 1896, one of eight children of a carpenter and his wife who had emigrated to Michigan a few years earlier from Danzig, Germany.

My father, Remembrance Hughes Lindsey Jr., was born ten years earlier into a wealthy family in Uniontown, Pennsylvania. As a child he was called "Hughes," the namesake of his great grandfather, a pioneer frontiersmen in western Pennsylvania although he later rechristened himself with the less formal "Robert." When it was my turn, I was baptized Robert Hughes Lindsey Jr.

After graduating from West Point shortly after the Civil War, my grandfather became a lawyer, then Fayette County District Attorney and later a local judge while investing profitably in coal mines in western Pennsylvania. In 1877, he married Elsie Evans Willson [sic]-- a second cousin of Woodrow Wilson. Her father, a Uniontown judge, was also a prosperous investor in local coke mines.

They had eight children including my father. When he was about fifteen, the family moved to Richmond, Virginia to be nearer the Willson side of the family (and not incidentally to enjoy the wealth yielded by a succession of legacies from both families). The family bought a commanding house at 600 West Franklin Street that was among the most prominent built after Richmond was sacked and burned during the final days of the Civil War.

Years later, the landmark mansion where my father grew up was restored to the standards of an historical museum and became an administrative building within the campus of Virginia Commonwealth University, where it is called "Lindsey House."

2

As was ordinary in wealthy post Reconstruction Virginia families, my dad was largely reared by an African-American nanny, a woman named Emma or Emmie, a descendant of former slaves. Despite his often-expressed affection for her, my father (perhaps reflecting the time and the region in which he grew up) was a bigot who named our black cocker spaniel "Nigger" and was forever hurling angry epithets about Jews. "Our country is being filled up and taken over by the riffraff of Europe and Russia," he told his children. Whenever we heard Kate Smith sing "God Bless America," he always pointed out it was written by a Jew, Irving Berlin.

It is impossible to pinpoint when he began his tailspin from scion of his prominent, wealthy Richmond family to a deadbeat alcoholic struggling to survive on Los Angeles' Skid Row.

His parents sent him to St. Paul's, a distinguished boarding school in Concord, New Hampshire, and he attended Princeton at the same time his kin, Woodrow Wilson, was its President, and then he was admitted to the U.S. Naval Academy at Annapolis. I never learned why he left both schools without graduating from either although my sister Jean believed he may have had to leave Annapolis after being infected by yellow fever during a summer midshipmen's cruise.

Also for reasons I do not know he was unable--despite trying multiple times, to enlist in the United States Army after the start of World I, although perhaps at 30 he was too old. After being rejected at home, he traveled to Toronto, lied on an application claiming to have been born in Canada and was mustered into the Canadian artillery and served in England, Belgium and France where he was felled on the battlefield by a cloud of poisonous mustard gas.

In a 1952 letter to my sister Jean, he said while he was on leave in London he visited an old friend from Richmond, Nancy [Nanny] Langhorne, then known as Lady Astor, a vicountess. She was the wife of Waldorf Astor, reputedly the richest man in England, the first woman elected to the British Parliament, and according to a 1919 *New York Times* profile, one of the most famous women in the world. She was one of Richmond's five "Langhorne Sisters" whose beauty, courtships, marriages and affairs were followed feverishly by readers from the decades after Reconstruction until World War II.

After learning that her friend from Richmond was in town she invited my father to a reception at her Thames-side mansion, Cliveden. Guests included the Prince of Wales and Mr. and Mrs. Winston Churchill. He recalled:

"I felt rather confused as I was dressed in my rank as a sergeant in the Canadian Artillery and all around me at the reception were 'top brass' Army and Navy but after Nanny introduced me as a lifelong friend of hers, everybody forgot rank…

"After the war when I finally got out of the Army hospital in 1919 [after a bout of influenza and after effects of the poison gas]] I got home just before my dearly beloved mother died, and I just could not stand the frivolous and silly set up of society in Richmond….. "

Turning his back on his birthright as a member of one of Richmond's leading families, it appears that he may have wanted some post war adventure and for more than a year found it as a civil engineer in primitive regions of Haiti, Peru, and Chile.

"I came west in 1920 to work with the U.S. Indian Irrigation Service in New Mexico and Arizona where I regained my health... I met your mother in 1921 while on a visit to Aguilar, Colorado. Since my marriage I haven't moved in the same circles I did as a single man, so had no chance to meet important people except my old friend, General Marshall."

After recounting the financial successes of his relatives, he wrote my sister: "I am sorry that I haven't been able, as your dad, to have the wealth my cousins and other relatives have; maybe it's true that 'a rolling stone gathers no moss,' but I wouldn't give up the memories my life has given me even though I cannot pawn them."

On August 10, 1921, a few weeks after meeting, my parents were married at a Methodist chapel in Trinidad, Colorado and honeymooned at his family's large lodge-style summer home nearby, the union of an aristocratic family from Old Virginia and a German working class immigrant family from Detroit. He was 35, she was 25.

Eight months later, their first child, my sister Catherine (nicknamed "Cappie") was born, followed two years later by Jean. I came along about fourteen years later.

It was not my mother's first marriage. Apparently the love of her life was an American soldier named Charlie who was killed in France. She spent the war waiting for him as a Yeomanette, one of America's first female sailors, at a naval station in Bremerton, Washington. After being widowed, she succumbed to a wanderlust and traveled throughout the West, supporting herself as a bookkeeper and spending many weekends marching as a suffragette. Then she met my father.

Dark haired and perhaps a little stout, she was pretty enough to attract my father, who by now had received his inheritance and was probably regarded as something of a catch. Unfortunately, they lost most of their fortune in the 1929 stock market crash and what was left went to Depression-era con men and bankrupt savings and loan banks.

Throughout their lives, there was a Mutt and Jeff imbalance to their horizontal appearance: my father, with thinning hair, a grey moustache and a slide rule seemingly forever in his shirt pocket, was slight and tentative, almost to the point of meekness; my mother was thicker, robust and more assertive. They both smoked prodigiously.

The family settled first in Burbank near Glendale, then Inglewood after my father was hired as an engineer for the Southern California Department of Water and Power to help design the Colorado River Aqueduct, a marvel of canals, tunnels, dams and pumping stations that propelled water hundreds of miles from the Colorado Rockies to the Los Angeles basin, helping transform it from desert to booming metropolitan region.

Some of my earliest memories are of watching him pour whiskey into his breakfast coffee. As I grew older, he began disappearing, having what my mother called "benders" or "blackouts," not showing up at his job for days.

After Pearl Harbor I seldom saw my dad—who was almost fifty when I was born-- without a glass of booze in his hands, usually complaining that he couldn't get in the Army and shouting drunkenly and argumentatively at my mother about her German heritage, inevitably variations of:

"You goddamned German" or *"You Nazi."*

Increasingly, he vanished into the shadows of Skid Row in downtown Los Angeles, usually unable when he returned to remember where he'd been or for how long. Once I boarded a Number 5 streetcar in Inglewood and rode downtown to a rundown hotel on Broadway found him and brought him home.

In the modern parlance of drug rehab I suppose my mother was an "Enabler," forever giving him "another chance." Perhaps she loved him and he loved her, although I don't remember witnessing hugging, kissing or other expressions of love between them. Whatever originally attracted them to each other, I never learned.

Midway through the war, out of patience with his blackouts and drinking, my mother divorced him and worked as a bookkeeper. He still tried repeatedly to enlist in the U.S. Army but at 54 was too old. Even appeals to General George C. Marshall, the legendary Army Chief of Staff, a close friend from Uniontown, failed to put him in a uniform, although Marshall helped arrange a government engineering job for him in the Panama Canal Zone. The divorce court ordered him to pay $75 a month in child support but my mother claimed he seldom paid it.

One of his sisters, Elsie Branch, the wealthy widow of a Richmond banker and a feisty beauty who'd been a volunteer ambulance driver in France during World War I, sent us occasional checks. In 1940, after my mother's father was killed by a hit and run driver, she inherited a two bedroom house he had built himself on Kelso Street in Inglewood and rented it for $65 a month to help make ends meet while we rented a smaller place or, later lived in the new trailer my mother had bought for us. When we were ever able to live in the house, my dad sometimes moved into our trailer parked near Hollywood Park.

Besides sending money, Aunt Elsie, a passionate show dog breeder and national officer of the Daughters of the American Revolution, made a proposition to my mother:

If she would send me to Virginia, Aunt Elsie, who was childless, would raise me as her son at Lower Tuckahoe, her eighty acre estate on the James River. As the last male in a line of Lindseys extending to before the Revolutionary War she said it was important for me to carry on the family name and make something of myself, and she wanted to help. I'm sure my mother didn't want me to leave but left the choice up to me: I could take Aunt Elsie's offer and live in Virginia if I chose.

Several times my mother telephoned or wired Aunt Elsie to say she couldn't cope any longer with my dad's drinking and wanted to put him on a Greyhound bound for Richmond. My aunt reacted with a coldness I never forgot. I remember my mother reading one telegram from Aunt Elsie while my father slumped in a living room chair, potted and glassy eyed.:

"UNDER NO CIRCUMSTANCES SEND HUGHES TO RICHMOND"

I *hated* her for that telegram. I told my mother If she wouldn't take my father, under no circumstances would I live with her.

A decade or so later, Aunt Elsie took her revenge. When she died, she cut me--and my sisters --out of her substantial estate while bequeathing a fortune to our Eastern cousins.

Still, curiously, my sisters and I may have been bequeathed a more lasting legacy than money: As children we had been constantly reminded that we were a part of the Virginia aristocracy, members of a genteel family that owned the grandest house in Richmond, whose ancestors helped organize the Whiskey Rebellion, fought in the Revolutionary War, were nation builders, judges, governors, lawyers and politicians . In other words, we were told we were *exceptional.* As odd and as foolish as it now seems, this unremitting repetition that we were special somehow persuaded me that it might be true.

3

As my father disappeared more often into the gutter, my mother tumbled into her own addiction, compulsive gambling. Three or four nights a week, we drove to Venice, a nearby beach town lined with canals from a long ago real estate development now bustling with Bingo parlors whose bright lights bathed the wide streets in a neon glow.

When my mom won at Bingo, she became giddy. When she lost-- sometimes as much as $60 in an evening-- she cried as we drove home. While she gambled, (no kids allowed in Bingo parlors) I wandered around Venice or took a nickel-a ride shuttle to nearby Ocean Park and rode the roller coaster or one of the other amusement park rides.

Looking back, it sometimes seems I was largely raised by my sisters, left to sleep at the home of Cappie or Jean and their husbands while my mother left town to join my father in another attempt at reconciliation, or she just left.

She loved to get in a car and go somewhere, anywhere. In 1947, she and I drove cross country to visit relatives in Michigan. And every few months she and four or five girlfriends drove to Death Valley, Arizona, Utah, New Mexico or into the California mountains. They called themselves "the desert rats."

While she was away, I stayed with one of my sisters or she asked my father to watch me.

It was then he began molesting me.

I don't remember how old I was when it began.

I do have a vision, emerging from deep in my brain, of a little boy in white jockey shorts and my father trying to stick his fingers into my crotch and his slurred, alcohol-infused sweet talk about how much he loved me.

I also remember running away from him and not always winning the race.

I remember him having me—this little kid in jockey shorts-- jump over a broomstick in a game, raising it higher and higher, and me trying to please him. Then he'd grab me and praise me for what I'd done and reach for my private parts and try to make me grab his.

It was terrifying.

After a few times, I sprinted to the bathroom and locked it. I was just a little kid. He pounded on the door drunkenly trying to get me to open it. When that didn't succeed, he pushed dimes and nickels under the door to persuade me to open the door. I can still hear the tinkle of the coins sliding through the crack under the door.

Why didn't I tell my mother? Why didn't I tell someone? I think it was maybe because I saw my father-- whom I loved-- as weak when fathers were expected to be strong and it was my job to *protect* him despite what he did, to hide what he did.   I rationalized: he only did it when he was drunk, so drink made him do it.

4

I was probably ten when my mother first said: "Bobby, you're the man of the house now…I know you'll never let me down."

What kind of weight is that to press onto a ten-year-old's slender shoulders?

When I was twelve, she promised me my own bedroom for the first time because our tenants in the Kelso Street house had given notice and we could afford to move in, thanks to her new job as a cashier at the Hollywood Park stables. But within a few days, she told me she was going to try again to reconcile with my father, and they moved to a trailer camp in Angels Camp in California's Gold Rush Country, where he'd landed a job as a surveyor. I moved in with Cappie and her husband and hitchhiked daily to St. John's, my Catholic grade school ten miles away in Inglewood.

Because of my father's continued drinking, this reconciliation didn't last much longer than the others. When my mother returned to Inglewood, she said we could still move from our trailer to the Kelso Street home but she would have to rent "my" bedroom to a border because we needed the money and my father wasn't paying child support. Hoping to lift my spirits, I suppose, she offered to turn our garage into a bedroom. It was more shack than garage, too small for a car, but I moved in with my clothes, bed, lamp and radio.

It was a short walk to St. John's from there, although my schooling was largely a succession of collisions with the nuns and priests who ran the place. The autocratic Irish-born priest who presided over the school, Father Reidy, expelled me three times. Each time my mother persuaded him to give me another chance or once, after one expulsion, spending some of her limited savings to send me to a Catholic military school in Los Angeles where I lasted three or four months but was soon back at St. John's in Inglewood. Once I angered Father Reidy so much he propelled me off of the front steps of the rectory with a hard kick of his right foot, ending my brief career as altar boy trainee. Still, I managed to graduate from St. John's and was accepted at Mount Carmel High School in Los Angeles a street car ride away whose $10 a month tuition my mother could afford. It was not only a *Catholic* high school but an *all boys'* school. I enjoyed working on the school newspaper but wanted girls in my life. After my freshman year, I talked my mother into letting me attend public school in Inglewood. Meanwhile, because we needed the rent from the Kelso Street house, we moved back to the trailer and my mother supported us with a bookkeeping job first at the Inglewood Plumbing Company, then in the offices of the Boilermaker's Union local.

5

By the end of the twentieth century Inglewood's population was almost exclusively African-American. In 1949 when I entered Inglewood High as a sophomore, the 50,000 or so residents were virtually all white, a few of them former members of California's last Ku Klux Klan chapter. Many of the most recent arrivals were part of the tide of emigrants from Middle West and Dust Bowl states who flooded Southern California during the Great Depression and World War II to work at local defense plants.

On one of my first days at Inglewood High, a short Italian kid came up and said:

"You new here?"

"Yeah," I said, and told him my name.

"Okay, Lins. Want to have lunch?."

He introduced himself as Sammy Bono, although he said his real given name was *Salvatore* Bono.

For a year or two, along with several buddies, we were the best of friends, hanging out, bowling, talking about girls, and being arrested, once for breaking into a classmate's family cabin at Big Bear Lake, once by a policeman who spotted a trumpet in our car and claimed it was stolen. We were taken to the 77th Street Police Precinct station in South Central L.A., where, after a few hours, I played my horn well enough to convince him I hadn't stolen it.

Wanting to fit in, I tried to restyle myself in the persona of what other kids derisively called a "hood," a Brandoesque rebel-- duck-tailed, oily-haired, leather jacketed, a wannabe auditioning for *"Rebel Without a Cause."* Trying to represent my lowlife tribe (our club called itself the "Merducos") I lost a couple of fistfights with rival gang members at Friday night football games while trying vainly to elevate myself in the Greaser hierarchy.

Bill Smith, the Boys' Vice Principal, commented while suspending me from school for three days for some forgotten infraction, said:

" Lindsey, I think your problem is that you want to be one of the boys."

He was right. I was a poseur, at heart inherently shy, introverted and insecure but pretending to be someone like Brando (without the motorcycle) in *"The Wild One"* because I needed to be accepted.

I was also a phony: I tried to hide from friends that I lived in the trailer camp.

Even in the lower middle class social order of Inglewood, trailer camp residents—many of them former Dust Bowl farmers-- were at the bottom.

When I went out with friends, I told them to drop me a few blocks from where I lived because I wanted to walk home. (Years later, at a high school reunion, two friends came up separately and said "Everybody knew you lived in a trailer.")

I also led a (brief) double life, trying to transport myself from trailer trash to Beverly Hills rich kid:

Inglewood High's football team competed in the Bay League which included several nearby high schools plus a couple of more distant schools in Santa Monica and Beverly Hills.

I traveled to games on the team bus as a sports reporter for the school paper and at one game in Beverly Hills met an attractive girl in the bleachers named Rachel. Impulsively, I introduced myself as "Barclay Addison Bates," a newcomer from "Back East" who would soon be transferring to Beverly Hills High.

I have no idea how or why I chose this alias but it must have seemed appropriate for a wealthy Beverly Hills teenage newly arrived from Back East, and for a couple weeks I tried to lead a double life under my new name. Twice, wearing a friend's expensive cashmere sweater, I took a bus—with two transfers—(I was too young to drive) from Inglewood to Beverly Hills and met Rachel for Cokes at a drive-in a few blocks from the school. We also talked a lot on the phone as I continued my pretence as time began to run ran out before my expected appearance in a Beverly Hills high school classroom. But . Rachel's mother picked up the phone when I called once and announced she'd checked at the high he school and couldn't find any evidence that I existed and told me never to call Rachel again.

That more or less ended the short life of "Barclay Addison Bates. I never spoke to Rachel again.

Sammy Bono was a fairly good singer and liked to compose music, and I began booking gigs for him at school assemblies and at Inglewood's local teenage club, sometimes calling myself his "manager."

But he was already moving on a different, much faster track than me:. By our junior year, he was sleeping with carhops in their twenties, ditching classes and drinking several nights a week. When I slept overnight at his house (his father, who was divorced, worked nights at an aircraft plant) he'd light up a cigarette, hand it to me and pour me a shot of his dad's whiskey. I tried but couldn't pull it off. I didn't like the taste of whiskey or tobacco.

With girls, I was terrified to pick up a phone and ask for a date. Sometimes when they answered, I hung up silently. Still, as it is for most teenage boys, it was a wonderful time of life, discovering girls who might like you as much as you lusted for them. As shy and insecure as I was, girls paid me enough attention to enable me to savor those years.

Like my father, my mother possessed quirky ideas about sex.

She seemed distressed when a girl occasionally telephoned, and when I started dating I suspected she was uncomfortable with it. When I was living in my garage bedroom, I invited a blonde named Carol over and we proceeded to do what teenagers do....kissing and petting. As we were going at it I heard the squeak of wood outside and knew someone was walking on the wooden porch outside the garage.

The next day, my mother didn't mention the previous night but said I didn't need girls from Inglewood High to do what I was doing. If I wanted to feel a woman's breasts, I could touch hers.

Girls, she said, didn't enjoy sex. Sex was "dirty." (Years later, when she visited my wife and I as newlyweds, she opened our bedroom door, flung off the blankets and said: "Bobby, are you still sleeping naked?")

6

During my first year at Inglewood High I took a journalism class from an English teacher named Bill Kamrath who didn't like me much, probably because I was still in my Greaser mode. But he took an interest in me because he thought he could turn me into a Lutheran— *his* church.

He did his best, but after seven years of parochial-school brainwashing and warnings from nuns and priests that I'd be incinerated in the eternal flames of hell if I didn't behave better, I wasn't a good candidate for any church. By 16 I'd decided not only Catholicism but all religions were a blend of fantasy, superstition, mythology and clerical intimidation.

Kamrath, who'd commanded a landing craft during the D- Day invasion of Normandy and was in his first year as a teacher, had had little experience in journalism beyond serving on his junior college's student newspaper. But he transmitted an almost religious zeal regarding the purpose and ethical values of journalism.

"The job of a journalist," he told us during the first week or so, "is to search for the truth. If any of you ever become reporters, you'll spend your life searching. And the *truth* is what you'll be searching for...

"Good journalists are skeptics not cynics; they're objective, not biased; they search for facts, not rumors, and take the facts they gather and try to make people make sense of them."

Midway through my junior year after working awhile as a reporter and sports editor on the student newspaper, *El Centinela*, Kamrath said he wanted to talk to me after class:

If I was going to get into college and make something of myself, he said I had to clean up my act and break away from Sammy Bono and the other purposeless friends I'd been running with.

Somehow he convinced me he was right. Abruptly, I turned my back on many of my buddies, some of whom never forgave me.

(Meanwhile, Sammy Bono, Kamrath's supposedly sure-to fail loser whose career I was "managing," dropped out of school and became *Sonny Bono*, Cher's husband, enormously rich pop star, future mayor of Palm Springs, California and future U.S. Congressman--and so ended my brief, tentative career in show business.)

After dumping my friends, I became a different sort of wannabe: a social climber seeking acceptance from the inner circle of respectable kids in the school while still trying to conceal the shame of being a trailer camp kid. My grades improved, I was elected to the Student Council, acted in the Senior Play and made the scholastic honor society.

(Sherman Thompson, one classmate, wrote in my senior yearbook: "*To Bob, who came up the hard way.*" Seeing his note, another classmate, Mary Raynor, wrote "*I agree with Sherm.*")

While working on the *El Centinela staff*, I decided I wanted to attend college and become a reporter. But like my mother, I was gripped by a wanderlust, desperately infatuated with seeing the world, mostly, I think, because of a series of novels I'd loved written by Howard Pease about a globetrotting itinerant seaman named Tod Moran.

My yearnings to travel became a part of my soul, an obsession.

In 1951, when I was 16, I flew from Los Angeles to San Francisco and back on a forged pass after convincing a classmate whose father worked for TWA to give me one of his family's expired annual employee passes.

With red ink, the aforementioned Sherman Thompson (a skillful artist), changed "1950" to "1951," and no one stopped me when I presented the pass at the gate and boarded a DC-3 with 19 or 20 other passengers. TWA officials in San Francisco were so taken by the charming son of their Los Angeles colleague (so they thought) that they let me bunk overnight in the airport crew quarters.

When I landed in Los Angeles the next day, I was busted at the airport but not arrested. My friend demanded the return of the forged pass, and I gave it to him with a great sense of satisfaction.

The flights only increased my determination to travel. A few weeks later during summer vacation, I got a job as a baggage handler for Western Airlines at the L.A. airport and flew on a legitimate employee pass to Salt Lake City, then to San Francisco.

Unfortunately, my boss discovered I had lied on my job application. I was only 16 when I claimed to be 18 and lost the job after only four months.

In my senior year, I was appointed co-editor of *El Centinela* with a non- "Greaser" new friend named Aaron Levy but made the mistake of igniting a cherry bomb in the print shop while we were closing the weekly edition and Kamrath fired me.

My mother pushed me to attend a local college, but Aaron and I—both from poor families-- chose San Jose State College about 400 miles north of Inglewood. Compared with other colleges it was cheap but reputed to have a fine school of journalism. Besides, something inside me wanted to put distance between myself and my mother who still kept calling me "the man of the house."

I thought 400 miles was distance enough. As it turned out, it wasn't.

Although my high school grades had improved during the final year and a half, they still weren't good enough, even for San Jose State, which rejected my application. I appealed and was accepted on probation.

Soon after my acceptance letter from San Jose State arrived my mother announced she was going to follow me to San Jose and establish a boarding house for me, Aaron and other students.

At its peak, she'd have six residents at her boarding house in San Jose, including me.

I never doubted she loved me and will be forever grateful she devoted much of her life to me, working to encourage and support me despite a husband who rarely supported her. I suspect she's partly the source, one way or another, of my drive to succeed. My sisters both claimed my mother "spoiled" me and they were probably right. She was a hard working Single Mother before it became common who was devoted to me, making sacrifices that propelled me forward. But can't a mother love, even smother a son too much?

I decided I had to move on, although it was painful for me and for her when I did.

My B+ average during freshman year ended my probationary status. The class I enjoyed most and earned the best grade in was American History, and I started thinking about becoming a history professor, not realizing until later the many parallels in the work of journalists and historians.

That spring I told my mother I had decided to move out of her boarding house into the Phi Sigma Kappa fraternity house. Disappointed, she closed her boarding house, moved briefly back to Inglewood, then rented a cabin in the High Sierras near Yosemite National Park.

I'd turned my back on her, but I'm sorry to admit I have never regretted it.

7

On a September evening in 1953 I turned and saw a flash of white angora wool, the collar on a navy blue sweater worn by a freshman named Sandra Wurts.

I looked into her face and said she looked familiar.

"Are you from LA?" I asked.

(A smooth way to open a conversation, I thought.)

"No," she said.

She said "no" again that evening when I walked her to a nearby beach and tried to kiss her.

As I did, she turned her head away from me and I said:

"What would you like to do?... *shake hands?*"

I don't know precisely when I fell in love with her... it may have been that night.

She was pretty, smart, sweet, shapely and funny and laughed at my jokes.

We met in a verdant woodland of pine and redwood trees on the Monterey Peninsula at an orientation weekend for San Jose State freshmen.

I was a sophomore 'counselor,' which gave me the right to wear a special gold and white school jacket (the school colors) and first crack at the freshman girls. Sandy was probably wise to turn me down that first night because when we returned to San Jose and began our classes, the rejection made me a persistent suitor. Later I learned her mother had told her daughters that girls should not express much interest in boys when they first meet because some boys, sensing triumph, won't return for seconds.

Our romance over the next three years was rocky, interrupted by three emotional breakups, Sandy's continued interest in other boys, and my getting "pinned" to another member of her sorority pledge class. (I was probably the only brother in the San Jose State chapter of Phi Sigma Kappa to ever ask his fraternity to serenade two different newly pinned girls at the same sorority house, Chi Omega.)

When at last we got engaged late during my senior year, the reaction of Sandy's mother, remembering our multiple breakups, was terse:

"*Oh no, Sandra,*" she said.

(It hadn't helped that on the day of my first invitation to her family home in Oakland I was arrested. I'd returned to San Jose after a week on the road as a door to door salesman to find a message to call the local police department. I did, a police car arrived and two cops with a bench warrant handcuffed me and drove me to jail because I'd forgotten to pay a traffic ticket I'd received on a previous visit to

Oakland. I called Aaron at the fraternity house and he bailed me out after I'd spent six hours in a cell, then called Sandy and told her I was going to be late for dinner.)

As a sophomore, I switched my major to history, my plans firming up to become a college professor.

Adding to about $20 a month I received from my mother, I supported myself as a dishwasher, janitor, camp cook for 18 hungry mouths in a U.S. Forest Service summer wilderness crew in the High Sierras, door to door salesman and many other jobs, including working as a teaching assistant to Political Science Professor William H. Vatcher, a prolific author and World War II aide to Admiral Chester Nimitz, who, bored with grading students' bluebook essay tests, hired me to do it.

In the winter of 1956, Sandy and I returned to the Monterey Peninsula where we'd met and I placed an engagement ring on her finger and we thought, "Wow, wouldn't it be wonderful if we could live here some day?"

Graduation approached. How does a soon to be married history major earn a living? Not easily I realized. Corporate recruiters visited college campuses each spring to interview graduating seniors and IBM and the Bank of America offered me jobs as a management trainee.

I applied to Stanford and with Vatcher's recommendation was provisionally accepted to attend graduate school leading eventually to a Ph.D. and a career as a history professor. After mentioning to Vatcher what I really wanted to do was see the world first, he offered to contact a friend in the shipping industry who could put me to work as an ordinary seaman on a freighter before starting graduate school. Within a few days, his friend sent me documents needed to apply for a passport, procure seaman's papers and get a berth on an upcoming six month voyage from San Francisco. When I told Sandy's dad I might take the job, he seemed delighted. "I'd do it," he said, making me suspect he was not anxious to lose his daughter or for me to become his son in law.

My mother attended my graduation at the San Jose State football stadium proud that I'd been president of my class and had received a few minor academic citations. She'd hoped I'd take a job near her and had even persuaded a neighbor who worked for the U.S. Forest Service, who'd earlier gotten me a summer job as a camp cook, to recommend me for a management trainee program for new college graduates. I told her Sandy and I planned to marry in a few months so I wasn't going to live with her. Wistfully, she replied:

" Here I put you through college and you leave me."

As I've mentioned, when I was a child, even when my dad was sober, I don't think I ever witnessed overt affection between them--it was mostly warfare I witnessed. But a year or so after my graduation I saw a snapshot with my father's arm around her, and before long, my father, finally off booze (thanks largely to Alcoholics Anonymous, and I suppose his determination and her patience) moved into the cabin in the High Sierras with my mother.

A year later -- 33 years after their wedding in Colorado--my mother and father drove to Reno and were remarried.

They at last found a bit of happiness together. At last, I thought, my father was the man of the house.

8

Instead of becoming a forester, ordinary seaman, history teacher, banker or seller of IBM electric typewriters, I took a job at the lowest pay on offer–as a country correspondent for the *San Jose Mercury-News*. It wasn't a *real* job: I was paid $250 a month as a non-employee-"independent contractor" to cover Gilroy, a farming town 30 miles south of San Jose. I jumped at the offer, a decision I never regretted, because from this apprenticeship, Sandy and I would go a lot of places.

Gilroy had fewer than 5,000 residents, a J.C. Penney, a Safeway, bank, mortuary, post office, Greyhound depot and several streets lined with single-story frame houses that were bordered by orchards, vineyards and fertile soil that produced mountains of garlic.

In later years, its citizens christened Gilroy "The Garlic Capital of the World." Then, Gilroy was just another agricultural town. Morning and night, a garlic processing plant broadcast such pungent fumes into the atmosphere that it seeped into my clothes and seasoned every breath I took.

When I arrived to start my new job in June, 1956, I'd had no training in journalism other than what I'd picked up in high school on the *El Centinela*.

My first byline as a professional reporter appeared over a story about horseshit. A truck loaded with manure stopped too quickly at the single traffic light in town, and the manure flew over the top of the cab, closing the town's main intersection for almost an hour.

That was the kind of news I reported from Gilroy

Sandy loaned me enough money for a down payment on a six-year-old Ford and we rented a $39 a month walk up apartment next to the post office. Four months later, September 29, 1956, we were married in Oakland.

From the beginning, Sandy managed to budget my slim salary with inspiration. For her birthday a month after the wedding, I surreptitiously bought her an Italian salami sausage (which I knew she liked from our days of courtship in San Francisco's North Beach Italian district), at Safeway for 69 cents as a surprise bonus birthday gift. Two days before her birthday I was typing a story in our bedroom when she looked at me quizzically and said: "We're missing 69 cents." I withdrew the salami from its hiding place and threw it *to*—not at-- her, convinced she really knew what she was doing when it came to keeping the books.

Within two or three weeks, she was pregnant and we were looking forward to producing our wonderful daughter, Susan. But a few months into her pregnancy, her doctor ordered her quarantined at the Santa Clara County Hospital in San Jose because she had been infected by the polio virus.

She was diagnosed with polio less than five days after we'd both downed a sugar cube doused with Sabin live polio vaccine.

The Sabin and Salk vaccines saved millions from polio, but for Sandy apparently a bad batch of the vaccine *gave* her polio. Still, after two or three months, we felt we'd dodged a bullet: . She'd been released from the hospital still feeling pain in her neck and spine, but was not paralyzed, and her doctors said the polio had healed and she'd fully recover.

They were wrong. More than 50 years later the polio returned, a painful, fatiguing disability now called "post polio syndrome."

Each morning, I left home to troll the "South County"-- my beat--for news. About 3:30 or 4, I sat down at a rickety Royal typewriter set up on a card table in our bedroom and wrote what I'd learned from local officials, cops and farmers. At 5:40, I sprinted down the stairs loudly and drove to the Greyhound station, greeted the 5:50PM bus for San Jose and handed the driver an envelope filled with my stories. Several nights a week, there was a City Council or school trustees' meeting, maybe a fatal automobile accident or brush fire or other event and I dictated the story directly to editors in San Jose, long before the Internet, Email, cell phones or even fax machines accelerated the process of news gathering.

From the beginning, I was a pest to these editors, lobbying for a transfer to a full-fledged staff writer's position at the San Jose headquarters, although our long term dream was to work on a newspaper in San Francisco, and our ultimate dream was to work there and live in a home overlooking the Golden Gate Bridge.

I learned a lesson in Gilroy that lasted a lifetime. Sandy and I were befriended by two neighbors, Rex and Melitta Vaughn, who were a few years older than we were. He was British, a mechanical engineer employed by a local manufacturer of food processing equipment; she was a surgical nurse and a native of Vienna. As our friendship deepened, we often had dinner at each other's apartments when virulent anti-Semitic attacks spewed out of my mouth as casually as if I was commenting on the weather. After I had repeatedly assailed "dirty Jews" and "Kikes" over the dinner table Rex said he wanted to talk to me privately, and he told me Melitta was Jewish, the daughter of parents lost in the Holocaust.

I was devastated by what I heard and what I'd done.

Except for a high school friend who was half-Jewish, nonreligious and thoroughly assimilated, Melitta was the first Jew I'd ever met. I suddenly realized I knew nothing about Jewish culture, history or religious beliefs or why I spewed out such toxic anti-Semitism. Melitta was one of our closest friends. She had introduced us to books, ideas, wines and European cooking in ways that changed our lives. The thought of hurting her ripped at my heart, but I realized what had happened: I'd become like my father.

No, I was becoming my father.

To recall how my remarks must have wounded Melitta hurts to this day. But the experience changed me: from then on I began judging people for who they were, not what they were.

I learned something else on my first job—the impact a newspaper can have on a community, even one as small as Gilroy: the local Rotary and Lions Clubs pressed me to cover their lunches, saying a newspaper was the only avenue they had to spread word of their good deeds; brides' mothers coaxed me to report their daughters' weddings or engagements, saying that only an article in the paper made the life-changing events seem official; when I reported how a planning commissioner had illegally voted to approve a building project on land he owned with his brother, my article killed the scheme; when a popular Gilroy-based California Highway Patrolman heard his estranged wife was having an affair and fired a bullet into her house I reported it—a story of only five or six paragraphs—and he was gone the next day after senior officers read the paper. Whether he was fired or sent to a remote CHP outpost, I never knew.

After more than a year and a half in Gilroy, I was offered a job with a regular union salary -- not in San Jose, but north of San Jose at the *Mercury-News'* "North County" bureau responsible for covering a chain of small towns—Sunnyvale, Mountain View, Palo Alto and Los Altos.

Sunnyvale was not the journalistic backwater Gilroy was, but it wasn't San Jose or San Francisco either.

Like Gilroy, Sunnyvale— epicenter of what the Chamber of Commerce called the "Valley of Heart's Delight"-- had long been a fertile farming and food processing community but it was changing rapidly. Every week acres and acres of prune and apricot orchards owned for generations by Italian families were being uprooted to make way for cookie-cutter subdivisions and low slung tilt up concrete buildings assembled into what developers called "industrial parks." During the fifties Sunnyvale's population had soared from fewer than 10,000 to more than 50,000.

Two weeks after I started the new job, our second child, Steve, was born and my new paycheck stopped after the San Jose Newspaper Guild, the union I had only recently joined, went on strike. I spent 129 days without a paycheck, with a wife, two babies and our first mortgage, surviving on meager union strike benefits.

9

On July 10, 1959, in the High Sierra village of Nippinwasee a few miles from the entrance to Yosemite National Park, my mother lifted my father, who was frail, incontinent and weakened by a stroke, on to the front passenger seat of their green Pontiac parked outside the mountain cabin they had shared since remarrying.

She was experiencing relentless pain after picking up a staph infection at a county hospital while recuperating with a broken hip.

She wove a garden hose from the Pontiac's exhaust pipe through a window into the cabin of the car, sealed the window with black electric tape, then settled into the driver's seat and turned on the ignition.

What happened next can only be surmised. The Madera County Sheriff's Deputy who investigated the double suicide concluded my mother at the last moment may have changed her mind about wanting to die. In the final seconds of her life, he said she had turned the ignition key, shut off the engine and opened the door beside her, then fell or pushed herself to the ground, but it was too late. The fumes of carbon monoxide had already done their work. A neighbor found her body sprawled outside the Pontiac and my father inside the car the following day. Both were dead.

In one of several notes my mother left on the dashboard she wrote:

"When this is read, we both hope to be dead. We cannot stand this existence any longer--sleepless nights and days of pain. So we are taking this way of ending it all....You have been a wonderful son to me and given me many happy years...I am so glad you have such a lovely wife, children and home and please hoard the happiness. It doesn't always last long...

"It breaks our hearts to leave you but today my pain is unbearable. Dad cannot get around much by himself and wants us to go together. If there is a God who put this burden on us, may He have mercy on us...:"

My father was 73 , my mother was 63 years old.

10

Somehow we survived my parents' suicide, the newspaper strike, the move to the Sunnyvale Bureau and Sandy's polio (or so we thought until it reappeared almost 50 years later).

With the strike over, I went back to covering the day in, day out business of local government around Sunnyvale, checking the police blotter and chronicling the minutiae of life as more and more orchards were leveled for still more subdivisions and industrial parks.

One morning I got a call from a man named William Shockley. He said he'd seen my byline and wanted to buy me lunch. I recognized his   name: Shockley had shared the Nobel Prize with two fellow Bell Laboratories researchers for inventing the transistor and the year before had established a company near his Palo Alto home. I had no idea why he wanted to see me.

The story he told over grilled hamburgers at Kirk's, a casual barbeque restaurant whose aroma of searing beef scented Mountain View and Palo Alto for blocks around, was both fascinating and sad:

After leaving Bell Labs, Shockley said he had returned to Palo Alto, the town where he grew up, to establish Shockley Semiconductor Laboratory and develop new electronic devices based on the technology he helped invent. His company had been making progress, he said, until eight senior engineers--whom he'd recruited after scouring technical universities across the country for their best and brightest graduates--resigned en masse and established a rival electronics firm financed by a large eastern company, Fairchild Camera and Instrument Corporation. He suggested I write an article about his company because he needed publicity to recruit engineers to replace them.

A slight, balding man who was about fifty, Shockley was full of himself, even cocky, but there was something lonely and touching about him. He seemed stunned and unable to understand what had happened to him, convinced he had been betrayed by a sinister conspiracy hatched by enemies on the East Coast.

I was puzzled why a famous scientist would ask *me* for help. He was honest: he said he needed publicity.

He was not only cozying up to a green cub reporter, he seemed to enjoy himself and after we finished our hamburgers he said he wanted to stay in touch and the next time he'd show me some magic tricks, his hobby.

I wrote a story about Shockley, but there was not a next time.

After the lunch, I called Fairchild Semiconductor and asked to interview one of the eight defectors. The group nominated its leader, Robert Noyce, to speak to me, and I was back at Kirk's for another hamburger, this time with Noyce, and I paid for the lunch.

The story he told differed from Shockley's.

According to Noyce, Shockley was an abusive, autocratic, egotistical, my-way-or-the-highway CEO who wouldn't consider his employees' opinions if they differed from his, and as a result they hadn't been allowed to pursue what they regarded as promising avenues of research.

Bob Noyce, like most of his partners, was in his twenties and full of dreams. He said Fairchild Semiconductor Corporation was initially supporting itself by manufacturing components for the guidance systems of Air Force Minuteman ICBMs, but beyond that it was researching designs for miniaturized devices in a new technology, "microelectronics."

A few electronic firms were already in Palo Alto – Hewlett-Packard and Varian Associates, for example –but it was the establishment of Fairchild Semiconductor Corp. by Noyce and his friends that was the seminal event in giving birth to the world's most fertile center of high tech industry based on exploiting the qualities of silicon, although perhaps Shockley could rightfully claim to be the father of the new industry, albeit a deposed one and whose late in life theories on racial superiority brought him lasting scorn and ridicule. In time, more than fifty companies would spring from the original "Fairchild Eight," dividing like runaway, hyperactive living cells and mutating into a huge industry in what was once called "the Valley of Heart's Delight.".

After meeting Shockley and Noyce I suspected I might be on to something important and decided to try to specialize in covering the new companies that were occupying the tilt up concrete buildings rising in the Santa Clara Valley.

For years, I was the only reporter covering this beat other than Don Hoefler, the editor of a San Francisco trade publication who in 1971 would be the first to call the Valley of Heat's Delight "Silicon Valley."

11

A friend from San Jose State mentioned after I'd been in Sunnyvale awhile that my collegiate mentor, Bill Vatcher, hadn't been seen at his office for several days and seemed to have vanished mysteriously. Since I'd last seen him, he'd written more books and twice ran unsuccessfully for Congress and did frequent interviews about international affairs. I called his office, confirmed he'd been missing for almost a week and wrote a story that ran across the top of the front page with a huge headline: *"Where's Bill Vatcher?"*

A day or two later, I heard a San Francisco radio station report that an apparently abandoned car, a yellow Opel, had been found near the YMCA building in that city and it was registered to Vatcher. I asked an editor if I could drive to San Francisco to learn what I could about what was going on. When I got to the YMCA, which was near n the Embarcadero a few yards from San Francisco Bay, I met two detectives coming out of the building who confirmed it was his car.

As I was leaving, I mentioned I had once worked for Vatcher, and one of the detectives said a man had been found near the Y a couple of days before without any identification and he was at the San Francisco General Hospital, alive but unconscious, his head brutally bashed in.

If it was Vatcher, could I recognize him?

Fifteen minutes later, I was looking down at an unconscious Bill Vatcher, his head wrapped in an oversized gauze turban that made me think of a mummy.

"That's him," I said.

With a little digging in the YMCA's neighborhood I discovered Vatcher had been leading a secret double life for at least two years, staying at the Y most weekends under an alias, William H. Peterson.

Vatcher"s head had been clobbered by someone, the detectives speculated, probably because he was a gay man in the then fully closeted (and persecuted) 1965 community of gay men in San Francisco. Or maybe he'd gotten in a dispute with another gay man, perhaps a gay hustler who'd robbed him, then beat him.

He died a couple of weeks later, never awakening from a coma. His killer was never identified. The detectives told me there had been a series of violent attacks on apparently homosexual men near the waterfront, and I followed up with several *Mercury-News* stories that began to open a window on the then little known clandestine gay culture in San Francisco.

My first- person accounts about identifying the man in the hospital bed and the college professor's double life made the front page beneath another huge headline.

"Now, all we have to hope is that Churchill doesn't die tonight, " John Howe, my boss, said as he showed me the Page One layout, consisting almost exclusively of my Vatcher stories.

In England, Winston Churchill was reported to be critically ill; if he died, the front page would have to be redesigned, diminishing the prominence of my scoop. Luckily (for me, and I suppose for him), Churchill survived the night and didn't die for another few days.

12

Reporting about the new high tech companies was more fun than covering planning commissioners or school trustees, and I wrote as much about them as I could. When Lockheed built a plant to build missiles and satellites in Sunnyvale, I started covering the burgeoning aerospace industry. In time, national publications --- *Missiles & Rockets, Aerospace Daily* and others--asked me to cover the region as their local "stringer," bringing us extra income and exposing my byline to a wider audience, and I morphed from City Council reporter to full time specialist on high tech companies with a weekly column.

Hoping for articles not filled with a cub reporter's errors, many scientists, engineers and CEOs sat me down and taught me how and why their new gadgets functioned, offering me one-on-one master classes taught by experts such as Noyce and Arthur Schalow of Stanford University, winner of a Nobel Prize in physics as co inventor of the laser.

Noyce explained Fairchild's goal was to drastically miniaturize electronic components, embedding ever smaller complete circuits in wafers of silicon, integrating potentially millions of transistors and other devices into spaces smaller than a thumbnail. He coined the term "integrated circuit," which over the next decades would become a ubiquitous component of everyone's life, from TV sets to cell phones to hearing aids to GPS systems-- to just about every other electronic device in the world, although during the early sixties he and the engineers and scientists he worked with often told me they didn't yet have any idea where their inventions would lead.

Still imbued with a dreamy wanderlust to explore the world, I discovered a fringe benefit of working in Sunnyvale when a public

information officer at the nearby Moffett Naval Air Station invited me
to fly to Hawaii aboard a Navy cargo plane, and I was soon on my way
to Honolulu. That trip was the beginning of a wide ranging
exploration of distant places. Husbands and fathers who flew the
Navy transports liked their families to read about their work, so I
began cultivating this understandable vanity and hitch hiking around
the world in military planes, sending articles home about San Jose-area
crew members from Europe, Puerto Rico, Tokyo, Alaska, Wake
Island, Okinawa and many other places.

In 1966 I was able to knock off both ends of the world
within a few months. In Spring, I flew close to the North Pole in a
Navy patrol plane that was hunting for Soviet submarines. In the fall, I
flew to Christchurch, New Zealand, then on to the South Pole.

As we approached the landing strip at McMurdo Sound in the
Moffett Field C-130, airport ground controllers in Antarctica reported
a "white out," a dangerous, disorienting atmospheric condition in
which the horizon is invisible because dense fog blanketed the earth,
including the landing strip. Our landing had to be made completely
on instruments.

When the pilot pushed the lever to lower the C-130's landing
gear and begin our final approach, it wouldn't move: the gear had been
frozen stuck by the subzero Antarctic cold. We couldn't turn back and
return to New Zealand because we didn't have enough fuel to get
home. A Navy enlisted man volunteered to climb down into the
landing gear wheel well to see what could be done to unlock the gear.
From inside the cabin, we listened to him pounding and pounding
the gear to break the hold of the ice. It lasted for at least six or seven
minutes as the plane circled McMurdo Sound. Finally his hammer
cracked the ice, he didn't fall out, the gear lowered, and we landed.

In those days few reporters visited the U.S. base in Antarctica,
which was operated jointly by the Navy and the National Science
Foundation, so they welcomed me, fed me well and flew me to remote
bases all over the continent, including a flight in a ski-equipped C-130
to the geographic bottom of the earth.

Built ten years earlier, the Pole Station was largely a warren of subterranean rooms dug into ice. I slept in a room that reminded me of living in a submarine except instead of water outside there were cold, howling winds that could wound and kill.

The next morning my candid portrait, as was customary for visitors, was taken next to a post painted like a barber pole marking the precise bottom of the globe: the South Pole--90 degrees South. The station commander, a Navy doctor, dutifully took the picture, then told me to race back to the ice caverns because my nose had turned white in the minus-50F degree cold, a case of frostbite that led to a lifetime of runny noses.

I returned to Moffett Field on a C-130, its passenger cabin empty except for me and 68 penguins bound for a New York zoo.

Because of the free military hops and profitable freelance market for stories about aerospace I added "aviation writer" to my brief as high tech reporter, even though I was far from passionate about airplanes, propellers, wind tunnels, jet engines, the shape of wings or anything else about aircraft except that they could take me to interesting places.

At a press conference about a new short take off and landing aircraft, the aviation reporter for the *San Francisco Call-Bulletin,* George Rhodes, pulled a letter from his coat pocket and showed me an invitation he'd received from British Overseas Airways Corp. to take a free trip, first class, to Hong Kong.

I couldn't believe it.

I wanted in on this.

I had become an "aviation writer" at an opportune time for a reporter who dreamed of exploring the world: the jet airliner had just been invented. Until then international travel was largely limited to the well to do or men and women in uniform. In the early 1960s, airlines began to launch jet service to destinations around the world and usually invited reporters to go along to write stories about their "inaugural" flights— referred to by me and my friends as "junkets."

The ceremonial-like inaugural flights usually included not only a free seat in the first class section of a new jet but several days of hospitality at five star hotels, banquets and VIP excursions in the foreign cities.

I joined and later became a national officer of the *Aviation Writers Association* and was perpetually on the phone to airline PR men (and women) expressing interest in their new routes. Before long, invitations for inaugural flights started arriving from BOAC, Pan Am, Japan Airlines, SAS, Lufthansa and other airlines for free trips that would take me in style--sometimes repeatedly-- to London, Munich, Copenhagen, Zurich, Prague, Paris, Berlin, Rome, Sydney, Auckland, Tokyo, the Fiji Islands and many, many other destinations.

I usually managed to send home articles that connected somehow to *Mercury-News* readers.

From London, to which I'd flown gratis on a BOAC VC-10 jetliner, I took a train to Scotland, rented a car and drove along the River Clyde to a place called Holy Loch to write about a ship moored there to support Polaris missile submarines – a Silicon Valley "local story" because the missiles were made in Sunnyvale by Lockheed.

In Hong Kong, I reported on new factories being opened by Fairchild and other San Jose-area electronics companies because of the plentiful supply of cheap assembly line labor – the earliest example of what was later called "off shoring" and "outsourcing."

As old time reporters will tell you, "if you look hard enough you can always find a local angle," and that's what I looked for.

The paper was tolerant about my travels, mostly I think, because I produced newsy stories...but more importantly, so was Sandy.

Never did she sacrifice more than during those years, when I was constantly in the air exploring the globe and she was raising the kids, alone.

During one trip to Australia, I interviewed the CEO of Qantas Airlines who told me something he shouldn't have: design details about a proposed supersonic transport that Qantas and other airlines were researching with Boeing. The specifications were supposed to be kept confidential, but he inadvertently spilled the beans. When I returned home, I called Bruce Webster, Qantas' PR manager in San Francisco who, along with his wife, Pat, had become social friends, and I mentioned what the CEO said and that I was writing about it for *Aviation Daily*, one of the publications I moonlighted for.

Bruce realized most of the technical details the CEO had revealed were not supposed to be published because of non-disclosure agreements signed by Qantas and other airlines. He called back and said both he and the CEO would be in trouble if executives at the other airlines discovered he'd leaked information about the design of the new plane (which ultimately was not built), and he asked me to exclude several details from my planned article.

Journalistically, it may not have been my finest hour, but I decided I could live with it and agreed to Bruce's request. I knew his boss had acted innocently – and besides, with the remaining information from the interview, I still had an interesting story.

Two years later, Bruce offered Sandy and me first class around the world tickets on Qantas. Only years later did he tell us it was in appreciation for what I'd done.

By 33, I'd accomplished my childhood dream to see the world, all for free. But my junketing would soon be over.

13

That's when *The New York Times* called.

To young journalists of my generation, *The New York Times* was the mountaintop, as hard to reach as the peak of Everest. On the few occasions I was at events covered by a *Times* reporter I'd furtively study him in awe like a little leaguer walking into a room and spying a member of the Yankees. Many were Ivy Leaguers and all were as smart as hell. One of the reporters I admired was Larry Davies, the courtly, grey haired *Times* Bureau Chief in San Francisco, who I'd occasionally see at news conferences, usually involving Silicon Valley or Stanford University.

In the fall of 1968, about six months after our around-the-world Qantas trip, Larry called and said the paper was looking for an "aviation writer" to work in New York, and he'd been asked by Richard Witkin, the transportation editor, who'd read some of my stories, what he knew about me. If I was interested in the job, Davies said I should send Witkin a letter along with clippings of several of my articles. I knew Witkin by reputation. A Harvard educated World War II B-24 bomber pilot, he was the most respected and influential aviation writer in the country. Within two or three hours of Davies' call, I sent Witkin a stack of articles regarding it as a hopeless gesture: I was from a Podunk city, a Podunk college and a Podunk newspaper, not even employed in the Podunk newspaper's main newsroom. It was an unattainable dream. But after a few days, Witkin called and asked me to fly to New York the following Monday to be interviewed for the job, suddenly making me feel like a small town altar boy being summoned to Rome to meet the Pope.

I made a plane reservation to New York for the following Sunday despite one complication: on Friday, I was scheduled for a vasectomy. But it was minor surgery and I decided I didn't need to postpone it.

In those days, the *Times* hired only a few reporters each year and took hiring very seriously. When I arrived at the newspaper's headquarters at 229 West 43rd Street I was scheduled to be interviewed by eight editors including several journalistic legends: James Reston, Harrison Salisbury, A.M. (Abe) Rosenthal, Arthur Gelb, Science Editor Henry Leiberman and Clifton Daniel, son in law of Harry Truman.

As I was waiting in the lobby that morning for the first interview, I could almost feel electric sparks in the air. Even well before lunch there were shouts of "Copy!" from reporters hunched over their typewriters and summoning copy boys to pick up their stories one page at a time, their voices raised against a symphony of clattering keyboards; 1968 was enormously busy in the news business as it was traumatic for the country: a presidential election, the spreading Vietnam War, the assassinations of Robert Kennedy and Martin Luther King Jr., the violent Democratic convention in Chicago, the spreading antiwar demonstrations.

While eavesdropping on some of the best news people in the country as they began the process of putting the next morning's paper together, I had the first "out of body" experience of my life: I was dazed thinking about what was happening; what the hell was I doing there, a kid (I was 33!) from the North County Bureau of the *San Jose Mercury-News* trying to crack *The New York Times*?

The first interview, with Salisbury, then National Editor, went fine. It seemed he wanted to look me over as quickly as possible, ask a few questions, then get on with gathering and editing the news on a busy day.

Next was Scotty Reston, a legendary columnist, then *Times* Executive Editor. As he leafed through my stack of clips he stopped at a story about a clandestine U.S. military base deep in the Australian Outback called Pine Gap that collected images from one of Lockheed's spy satellites. I'd reported the story after taking a BOAC inaugural flight to Sydney.

He seemed puzzled that a minor newspaper like the *San Jose Mercury-News* could fund a reporting trip into the heartland of Australia.

"Did your paper send you or were you on a junket?"

Trying unsuccessfully to avoid blushing, I answered it was a junket.

While he read on, I imagined the most famous newspaper journalist in the country -thinking that this guy should never be hired at the *New York Times*. In hindsight I suspect he wanted to remind me of something I already knew: *Times* reporters did not go on junkets or accept free *anything*.

14

"Are you a science writer?," Reston asked as he studied several stories I'd written about the high tech industry.

"I write a lot about science and technology," I said, than volunteered gratuitously: "I think it's possible to write things about science and technology in a way that can satisfy both readers who don't have a lot of scientific background and the scientists you're writing about."

He looked at me, then back at the clips.

"You shouldn't worry what people you write about think about you."

Twice I'd said the wrong thing. There goes the job.

While Reston continued reading my stories, I studied the reporters, rewrite men and women and editors preparing the next morning's paper, then felt a trickle of moisture on my leg.

I realized immediately it was blood or pus dripping out of my scrotum. Tape holding the gauze dressing over the incision made during my vasectomy three days earlier had come loose and was rolling down my leg, tickling me and leaving a trail on my pants.

I sat still as the interview continued, covering my crotch with my hands while fearing that as soon as I stood up everyone in the room would see my trousers smeared with dark blood.

Reston finished and dismissed me politely and said Clifton Daniel was waiting for me. I found the employee rest room, opened a cubicle, sat down and stuffed wads of toilet paper into my crotch. Already blood had stained my pants; all I could do was hope it blended into the brown fabric and nobody noticed.

When it was his turn to interview me, Gelb, the Metropolitan Editor, asked how much I expected to earn at the *Times*, I waited a moment before answering. In fact, I would have been glad to work at *The New York Times* for nothing, but came up with a figure: $20,000 a year, about $7,000 more than I was earning at the *Mercury-News*. He didn't respond.

My last stop was a second interview with Dick Witkin and also Hank Leiberman, then science editor but previously a foreign correspondent and China specialist. I think I made a good impression, but never forgot one of Leiberman's remarks:

"I have several rules about the New York Times. One is that sooner or later it will break your heart."

At the end of a very long day, I was offered the job at a salary a shade less than $20,000.

I called Sandy, told her I had the job and would have to start work in New York in less than three weeks.

She wasn't happy.

She hated the thought of leaving California. I flew home, sold our cars (including my favorite, a classic racing green Morgan roadster), and helped Sandy start packing. When I returned to New York, I rented a foul, urine smelling room at the *Hotel Dixie* across 43rd street from the newspaper and started work. Sandy sold the house by herself, finished packing and tried to placate the kids, who were as unhappy about leaving California as she was.

On my first day at the paper, I passed a physical exam and was given a New York City Police Department press card called a "shield" and a *New York Times* Air Travel Card, enabling me to charge airline tickets to anywhere in the world. Then I began a week of orientation, sitting with different editors each day .

It didn't take long to discover a major transformation was beginning to occur at the Grey Lady of 43rd Street.

15

For decades—or for that matter, probably through the entirety of its existence—the *New York Times* had been an "editors' paper." In the newsroom hierarchy, reporters were less than equal, just a few rungs above copy boys.

Editors had the ultimate word on everything. They stressed complete, accurate, ethical reporting, but almost always deleted colorful, unorthodox or imaginative writing. It was this tradition that arguably created the newspaper's reputation as the dull Grey Lady of 43rd Street.

On my second day of orientation I was invited to the "Page One Meeting" a few minutes before 6 pm, when the top stories of the day were laid out on a dummy front page, and I witnessed a tectonic event in the glacially slow-moving history of the newspaper.

Only a few top editors – known collectively as "the Bullpen"-- participated in this meeting. It was the unchallenged fiefdom of Assistant Managing Editor Theodore M. Bernstein, a former copy editor, nationally known author of books on grammar and word usage, Columbia University professor of journalism, and top dog enforcer of style and good taste, kingpin of the newsroom.

He had ruled the Page One Meeting as an absolute monarch for years. But in the fall of 1968, he made the mistake of underestimating Abe Rosenthal, who had been recently brought home from a distinguished overseas reporting career to become Associate Managing Editor, outranking Bernstein, with a mandate from Publisher Arthur ("Punch") Sulzberger to make the paper more interesting, lively and better written.

As I sat on the sidelines watching, Bernstein as usual decreed which stories would go "out front" the next morning and after filling out a dummy layout of Page One with his choices he said the meeting was over. But Rosenthal didn't move; he shook his head and ordered what he said was a well written feature article Bernstein had rejected for Page One to be displayed in a prominent spot at the bottom of the page.

Bernstein said "no." Rosenthal said "yes," and he prevailed.

I'd witnessed a changing of the guard at the seat of one of the world's most influential journalistic enterprises.

During the next few years Rosenthal and his friend, Arthur Gelb, would preside over an even more sweeping remake of the paper, but on my orientation day I watched as the center of power begin to shift palpably at the *Times*.

Like all new newsroom employees, I was on probation for six months. And during those six months I woke almost every morning with a case of diarrhea, my body telling me I was certain to be fired that morning because I didn't belong at *The New York Times*. Everywhere I looked were people brighter than me, editors and reporters, competitive Ivy Leaguers, smart men and women my age or younger eager to keep me off the front page, unimpressed with my origins in Podunk. One evening I discovered I was even a greener yokel than I realized. Back home, I'd written an article for the *Mercury-News* about the owner of a Greek restaurant, Louis Gundunas, who each night entertained customers with a "table dance." Against a background of Greek music, Louie danced around the dining room, then bent down and lifted a table off the floor with his front teeth and continued his dance, swaying to the rhythms of the music.

About the time I landed in New York -- Sandy and the kids were still in California--Louie contacted me and said he was also in the city because he'd been hired to perform the table dance in a new musical, "*Zorba.*" We had dinner and afterward he invited me to a party for the cast at the apartment of one of its members.

He led me around the room, introducing me to everyone. When I got to one friendly man, I asked, "What part do you have?"

He very kindly said, "I'm the producer."

I should have been embarrassed, but was too dumb to be. He was Harold Prince, probably the most famous Broadway producers at the time, and I had never heard of him. That's how the yokel from Sunnyvale made a splash in the big city.

Within a few weeks, Sandy flew to New York briefly and we leased a furnished house in Darien, Connecticut, a 55 minute New Haven Railroad commute to Grand Central terminal.

On Christmas Eve, after enduring glares of family and neighbors angry I was taking the family to New York, we flew East, arriving during a snowstorm. Especially to Californians unaccustomed to snowstorms, it was bitterly cold and unpleasant , nobody was happy and we had to drive to our new home over slick, ice-covered roads. As we left Kennedy International Airport, we started looking for a roadside restaurant on the way to Darien.

Everything was closed. As we inched into the waterfront commuter town torrents of sleet rocked our rented car, When we hit a pack of black ice the car slid like a toboggan over the slick street until smashing into a post, although luckily none of us was hurt.

Despite a dented front fender, the Oldsmobile was still running, until not far from our new home, I saw a neon sign:

"PIZZA"

Happy, I pulled up to the restaurant, got out of the car and pushed my way through the sleet. As I reached the front step, a window shade on the front door began descending and a sign, "CLOSED" materialized.

I knocked on the door, and a man opened it.

"Could we get some pizza, please?," I asked.

"It's Christmas Eve," he said, and closed the door.

I knew then how Joseph and Mary must have felt when they were told there was no room at the inn on Christmas Eve.

We found our rented home and went to sleep; there was not much choice; the rented furniture did not include a TV set. Christmas Day we spent watching a Beatles movie, *Yellow Submarine,* at a theater in nearby Stamford.

After the holiday, the kids started school in Darien and I returned to work in New York, writing stories almost every day-- about airlines, air fare wars, the newly developed Boeing 747, strikes by air traffic controllers, congestion at the city's three jetports and the search for a site for a fourth.

Few were flashy stories, the kind noticed by editors. I suspected Witkin was disappointed with the new reporter he'd found in California. It didn't help when I made a couple of factual errors in my articles and learned quickly that even the most insignificant error in the *New York Times* draws a chorus of complaints, not only from bosses but readers. Subscribers took mistakes very seriously. I started waking up with a vision of millions of people picking up their paper every morning just waiting to point out a mistake in one of my stories. The errors I made were not serious...a misspelled name, an incorrect date perhaps--but I quickly learned to double and triple check every word, still afraid of being sent back to Sunnyvale.

The *Times* newsroom stretched an entire block between 43rd and 44th streets just off Times Square and was divided into sections for the three central divisions of the daily paper: the National, Foreign and Metropolitan desks.

Metropolitan Desk reporters, who covered local news from the city and suburbs, worked at long desks seated at typewriters facing 43rd Street. In the front row senior position were well known rewrite pros like Homer Bigart and Peter Khiss.

A couple of hundred yards away-- isolated at the other end of the room, their windows overlooking Broadway theaters and 44th street, were a dozen or so tired-looking reporters, some of whom occasionally pulled a liquor bottle from a drawer and drank from it. Several had famous bylines. They were men and a couple of women mostly in their sixties who had spent much of their lives covering exciting, historic events, the Lindbergh trial, the Spanish Civil War, the D-Day landings at Normandy and the fall of Berlin.

But after a million deadlines and bylines and glamorous careers as globetrotting correspondents, they'd been returned to New York burned out, reduced to writing-- if they did any work at all -- about mundane topics...perhaps the opening of a school or the arrival of a new ocean liner in New York harbor. Perhaps elsewhere they would have been considered "deadwood," even lazy, and been retired after a brief cocktail party upstairs. But the *Times* then was a generous employer and kept them on, even treating these old warhorses with kindness and affection.

Although I reveled in the war stories the old pros told me as they held court at the back of the City Room I decided I never wanted to close out my life that way.

I vowed never to be an "old" reporter.

16

After six months, I passed my probation and Abe Rosenthal, when he broke the news, said "we're now married to each other."

In other words, the Newspaper Guild could made it difficult for *The Times* to fire me now.

I started joining colleagues who'd been among my journalistic heroes at two martini lunches at Sardi's, the showbiz restaurant next door to the paper. In hindsight, I was probably still hoping to become one of the boys.

Arthur Gelb, some of my colleagues said jokingly, was the only man in New York who "can run amok sitting down."

He was a great editor but spewed out story ideas (some good, some not so good) like an erupting volcano, prompting me to begin running the other way when he approached me in a hallway or at the men's room urinal, fearful of being diverted for days by still another questionable Gelb project. Still, he gave me good advice:

"Remember, you're not just an *aviation* writer. You're a *transportation* writer. Think broadly. *Write about anything that moves.*"

Sandy and I bought a home on two acres in a stunning wooded area of Westchester County near the Connecticut town of New Canaan about fifty miles north of New York City, and I became like one of those dark suited briefcase-toting Manhattan-bound train commuters often portrayed by Jack Lemmon or Gregory Peck. Until we bought a second car, Sandy drove me to the New Canaan railroad station every morning. I bought the *Times* and a cup of coffee and completed the two hour, one way trip between home and office. At night, it was another two hour trip home and Sandy met me at the station and after she got a job we could afford to go out to dinner after she met me. True, it was a long commute, but local schools were good.

Almost from the first month, I began agitating for a transfer to California. Five correspondents were based there, three in Los Angeles and two in San Francisco, but vacancies rarely occurred.

Naively, I approached Gene Roberts, the National Editor who supervised these bureaus, and said I wanted to be considered if one of the jobs ever came open.

A slight North Carolinian with a broad twang reaching back to his Southern roots, Roberts looked up at me with a languid expression from an article he was editing as if seeing me for the first time, (which may have been true), and said in his characteristically slow drawl:

"*Everybody* wants to go to California."

He more or less dismissed me, then looked up again as I started to walk away.

"*Write yourself on to the front page,*" he said. "Then we'll talk."

One evening shortly after I'd completed my probation, I caught the 7:05 PM Penn Central commuter train from Grand Central Terminal bound for Stamford, Connecticut; as usual, I got off at Stamford and jumped on to a three-car shuttle train that connected it to New Canaan on a spur line that passed through several residential neighborhoods. Sandy was waiting with our car in New Canaan.

I was engrossed in a book when the train slammed head- on into a three-car train coming from New Canaan. The thunder of the collision was heard fifteen miles away. Sparks lit up the sky for blocks. Both of the colliding trains were stopped instantly in their tracks, but I wasn't: the impact flung me out of my seat as if I'd been fired by a cannon. After looping head over heels several times, I landed on the hard back of a seat seven rows in front of mine, unconscious with my head bleeding and two ribs cracked. Within a few moments, another passenger helped me to my feet and we began leading others out of the smoking train.

Four people were killed in the crash, dozens injured, including me. As soon as I had my wits, I realized I'd better call the paper to report the train wreck. I asked one of the people in the neighborhood who'd been drawn from their homes by the noise of the collision if I could use their phone and reported the crash to the rewrite desk in New York. Only later, when I was at a hospital, did I realize my pants and shorts had been shredded during the accident, and when I'd asked a woman to use her phone I had exposed her to a lot of my flesh.

A day later, I got a letter from Managing Editor Clifton Daniel:

"Dear Bob:

We have heard how gallantly you performed on the New Haven train wreck story in spite of your own painful injuries. Your behavior was in the best journalistic tradition, and we want you to know that it was greatly admired by everyone here."

Following Gelb's advice, I wrote about anything that moved. Not just supersonic airliners, but about the New York City subways and commuter trains, new rapid transit systems around the country, ferry boats, ocean liners, even the plight of pedestrians who lacked public transportation in an isolated Appalachian hamlet called Baptist Ridge. I remember the moment when I first thought I might succeed at the *Times*, after writing a seemingly routine front page story that began this way:

The chartered-bus crash that killed seven children near Allentown, Pa., last Wednesday has spotlighted wide gaps in Federal and state laws regulating the nation's booming charter bus business. It has also raised new concern among Government safety experts over the "crash-survivability" of modern buses." "

David Jones, Gene Roberts' deputy, approached my desk that morning, complimented me on the story and said, "We should have thought of that." Roberts and Jones were trying to introduce a new consciousness to national reporting, best described as "trend stories." Roberts cited the exodus during and after World War II of millions of African- Americans from the South to Northern cities, a sweeping event largely unreported at the time that occurred over years, not days; it wasn't a "spot story," as reporters called one-off events. In Roberts' views, there were other broad trends, perhaps not as significant as the African-American migration, but nevertheless still important and he wanted *Times* reporters to report them.

I tried to follow his suggestions and my stories began landing regularly on the front page. When I won a Publisher's award for one story my picture appeared on a bulletin board in the City Room underneath a profile written by Dick Witkin:

When Bob Lindsey was in high school in Inglewood, California, he ran around with what, in those times, was pegged as a 'fast" musical crowd that drew much of its inspiration from a student named Sonny Bono. One of his teachers told Bob he might get somewhere in the world if he buckled down to work and left the Bono orbit, which he did.

Bono turned out to be the Sonny of the husband and wife rock singing team of Sonny and Cher, which prompts Bob to say:

"I don't know if I did right. Look at him!"

One can only guess what sort of success Bob might have had in the pop music field. But to judge by the crisp, originally-phrased tones he constantly gets out of his busy Underwood, he made no serious mistake giving up the musical crowd for the news business.

Bob was discovered by The Times much the way Tommy Heinrich was found by the Yankees. Baseball scouts came across the talented outfielder hitting some long balls for an obscure softball team. Bob was discovered, with some scouting help from Larry Davies, covering the aerospace beat for a relatively obscure (at least to eastern big leaguers) California paper, the San Jose Mercury News.

Bob jumped at the chance to join The Times even though he knew it would be something of a wrench giving up the sun-soaked living style of his San Jose home (complete with swimming pool) for life in the harsher Northeast.

And so it was. He and his pretty and petite wife, Sandra, had to stray into exurbia (a New York town across the state line from New Canaan, Connecticut) and a two hour door to door commute to find a house (split ranch without pool) they liked at a bearable price.

In describing their gradual adjustment to the new life style, a close friend says:

"You can take the boy out of California, but you can't take California out of the boy."

There's a lot of outdoor cooking at the Lindsey household – a quartet that includes a 13 year old girl and 11 year old boy. The emphasis is on California-style menus ("they use a lot of pineapple, for instance," says a frequent visitor) and the best in California wines. Sandra, a Medford, Oregon girl he evidently met in college—is an excellent cook, and Bob fancies himself "a fairly good amateur chef."

Bob also has brought east a California-instilled taste for sports cars as well as a continuing interest, despite the split from the Bono crowd, in music – all kinds, from musical comedy to classical. A good part of the Lindsey entertainment budget goes for discriminatingly-picked restaurants and theater and movie tickets.

Bob was born in Glendale, California, 35 years ago. By the time he was through high school and ready to enter San Jose State College, he had had the sort of extracurricular job exposure that sounds like a satire on the education of a future newsman. He ran a window washing business, was a window dresser and janitor in a liquor store, sold programs and food at the Los Angeles Coliseum, and led a swing band that played at high school dances.

He's now proving that all these jobs can be great preparation for being a newsman at The Times.

During the nearly seven years I worked in New York, I learned the *Times* could be a brutal workplace, unforgiving of errors by editors as well as reporters. Ted Bernstein, the long time editorial monarch, lost his battle with Rosenthal and was moved out of the City Room to a tiny office he shared with me and Dick Witkin, who'd been one of his protégés. Clifton Daniel, the patrician Southerner who married Harry Truman's daughter, was demoted by *Times* Publisher Punch Sulzberger because of a dispute over staffing the Washington Bureau and was reduced to interviewing cub reporters like me about stories they'd written for *The Times*' classical music station, WQXR; after being humbled, he was eventually rehabilitated and appointed head of the Washington Bureau. Science Editor Henry Leiberman lost his job over a different issue, fulfilling his prediction that The *Times* would eventually break your heart.

The years in New York were tough on Sandy and the kids.

Even though I'd made them move across the country, made them start new lives while I hung precariously to a job I didn't think I would keep, they gave me unfailing support. I suppose every father thinks their children are the best in the world. Mine were. Susan and Steve were intelligent, kind, empathetic and sweet children but also independent minded creatures willing to take on Sandy or me if they thought we were wrong. Biased as I am, they were both fusions of Sandy and me, our best characteristics and perhaps some of our lesser ones.

17

"Guess what?," I said. "Bob Wright died"

In the office of the *New Canaan Advertiser,* the weekly newspaper where she worked in the business office, Sandy clutched the phone and let out a yelp.

"What's happened?," her office mates asked.

"Bob Wright died!."

"Who's Bob Wright? And why are you so happy?"

Wright, a specialist on economics, was one of three correspondents in the Los Angeles Bureau of the *Times,* and as repulsive as it may seem now, I'd been waiting for someone to die so I could be transferred to California. Dave Jones, the Deputy National Editor, and I had conferred for months at lunch plotting a route for me to become a National Correspondent, and Wright's death (he was known to have a troubled heart) had paved the way.

Coincidentally, the day before Wright died, John Lee, the *Times'* Deputy Business and Financial Editor, took me to lunch at Sardi's and offered me a choice of two jobs, as his deputy in New York or as business/financial correspondent in London, a job coming open soon.

Just two years earlier, we'd built our dream house, a beautiful cedar and glass home on six lakefront acres in northern Westchester County in a rural enclave called Waccabuc; Sandy was enjoying her job at the *Advertiser* and Susan and Steve were happy at very good public schools. Still, there was never a doubt among any of us about choosing to return to California.

We flew West, bought a house overlooking the Pacific an hour's drive from the Bureau in downtown Los Angeles. Susan entered the University of California Irvine, and Steve attended a nearby high school before moving on to the University of Southern California.

I dove into my new assignment, trying to explain to New York readers what was happening on the Left Coast.

A few months after we settled in, the Washington Bureau tipped me that former President Richard Nixon, who was in self imposed exile down the coast in San Clemente, was about to make his first public appearance since resigning the presidency fourteen months before, at a golf tournament held by the International Brotherhood of Teamsters, the only major union to support him as president. The site was a resort called LaCosta about 30 miles from San Clemente that had been in the news recently because of alleged ownership ties to organized crime.

I booked a room at the resort and learned from an employee where Nixon was likely to arrive with his Secret Service protectors. The prospect of landing the first interview with Nixon since his resignation was exciting.

By then I'd identified other golfers who'd already arrived for the tournament named in honor of Frank E. Fitzsimmons, the union's president, and they included several mob figures who were suspects in the recent disappearance of former Teamsters boss Jimmy Hoffa.

When his black Secret Service Cadillac pulled up at the appointed place and Nixon stepped out of the car, I left the shelter of a tree where I'd been waiting and said, "Mr. President, I'm Bob Lindsey from *The New York Times*. May I ask you a couple of questions, please?"

He seemed stunned by my sudden appearance and started backpedaling as if he was on a bicycle going backward, retreating into the limo he'd just exited. But as he started to sit down he seemed to regain his wits, shifted gears and began walking forward again and I said, "Mr. President, how are you feeling?"

"I'm just fine, and I'm going to play good golf today," he said before climbing into a golf court driven by Fitzsimmons, who drove away while security officers with long arms barred me from following the cart.

I've always maintained this was Nixon's first newspaper "interview" after his resignation. My editors didn't agree that the few words we exchanged constituted an interview but they did run my story under a big headline on Page One.

Many New York editors believed California was a land of kooks and cultists, and it was easy to meet their expectations; I could have made a full time career simply writing about cults and New Age religious con men and women, but I went after a broad range of subjects, anything that interested me: California's economy, agriculture, smog, traffic and water wars; its aerospace and electronics industries, its booming population growth and late seventies' real estate bubble. After awhile, I started gravitating occasionally to stories about Hollywood and film making, confirming what I overheard one of my office assistants tell a friend on the phone: "Everyone New York sends out here wants to write about the movies."

One of my first major reportorial targets was Mary Pickford, the silent screen actress who was America's first movie superstar. She hadn't been interviewed by a newspaper since before World War II. She was 82, a recluse, and still living in a legendary Beverly Hills mansion called Pickfair, where for more than a decade she and her husband, Douglas Fairbanks, entertained lavishly, the most famous and richest movie stars in the world.

A canny businesswoman who made millions in the movies, then millions more in real estate, she lived at Pickfair with her third husband, actor and band leader Charles "Buddy" Rogers.

In early 1976, the Academy of Motion Pictures Arts and Sciences decided to present a Life Achievement honorary Oscar to her at the upcoming Academy Awards ceremony. It would be her second Oscar; the first was in 1929.

With the special award coming, I naively thought I could easily arrange an interview with her.

I located her business manager, Matthias Kemp, in a Beverly Hills office building where he looked after her real estate holdings, and he was genial and polite but adamant:

"Mary doesn't do interviews anymore," he said. "She wants people to remember her just as she was. I think her last interview was in 1937."

That was a year after she divorced Fairbanks, whose adulterous philandering in Europe destroyed their marriage.

Disappointed, I returned to the Bureau and mentioned my conversation with Kemp to Jerry Flint, an editor in New York.

"Send her flowers," he said. "Women always like that."

At one of Beverly Hills' more fashionable florists, I selected two dozen red roses and watched its delivery van head for Pickfair.

The next day Kemp called and said Mary was so pleased by the roses that she'd consented to an interview, and he invited me to lunch at Pickfair, launching me on an adventure with echoes of "Sunset Boulevard," the film about a faded silent film star who never accepted her career had ended.

Pickfair (named by combining Pickford and Fairbanks) lived up to its reputation: It was huge, with 22 rooms covering more than 20,000 square feet and decorated with French, English and Oriental antiques and a wall of Rodin sketches. All around me were expensive objects d'art from across the globe. The home commanded six hilltop acres and had a pool, tennis courts and large guest house.

Kemp and Buddy Rogers greeted me and led me to the dining room through a saloon that seemed transplanted from a western movie and dominated by a bar Fairbanks had imported piece by piece from a Gold Rush ghost town.

When we reached the dining room I noticed the table was set for three.

Where was Mary?

"We'll talk to her after lunch," Rogers assured me.

As one of Pickfair's servants put a bowl of creamy leek soup, then salad nicoise in front of me, Rogers reminisced about some of the guests who'd dined at the table where I was having lunch: Charlie Chaplin. F. Scott Fitzgerald, FDR and Eleanor Roosevelt, William Randolph Hearst and his mistress, Marion Davies, Noel Coward, Albert Einstein and many others, including gangster Bugsy Seigel. He talked about visits to Hearst at San Simeon, his lavish estate up the coast, and said Hearst gave his guests sterling silver or gold Dunhill cigarette lighters.

Over the salad, he explained I wouldn't actually be *seeing* his wife. But I'd be able to interview her via a telephone extension from a room directly next to her bedroom and I'd hear her voice from the bedroom.

"Mary wants people to remember her as she was," he said, referring to the sweet, spunky, wholesome character with golden curls she played in more than two hundred movies between 1909 and 1933. "She thinks people will expect her to look like she did then, the girl with the curls."

With lunch over, Rogers led me up Pickfair's central staircase and at the top shouted *"Mary, Bob's here."*

"Okay, Buddy," a disembodied voice from behind an open door answered.

He picked up a telephone extension and handed it to me, and so began a forty-five minute conversation during which Mary was lucid and articulate some of the time while drifting at other moments into a cloud anchored in a world sixty years before.

"I could still be on the screen, you know," she said. "I'm far from being elderly. And I'm sturdy. I'm ready to go back to work, yes I am.

"You know, I'm of English and Irish heritage, and we know how to work hard. Why I used to make two pictures a week. I loved my work and I miss it very much."

"I had a beautiful career," she added, "and it was fun."

When she repeated her determination to make another movie "as soon as tomorrow," her husband, sitting beside me, tried unsuccessfully to suppress a soft laugh, and she heard him.

"Buddy's laughing at me," she said.

"He's laughing *with* you," I said.

"He'd better not be laughing *at* me. I really want to go back to work, and he knows I could do it."

After awhile, Rogers nodded, indicating it was time to wrap up.

When I said goodbye, she said, "Bob, be sure to give Buddy your telephone number so we can talk again."

The story about Mary was played prominently by The *Times*. A couple of days later, she sent me a warm note expressing her pleasure with the article and noting several of her old friends had called to say they enjoyed it. I framed the letter and put it up on the wall of my office and started gathering material for my next story.

That was it, or so I thought.

About a week later, she called me at home one evening and told me again she'd enjoyed the article.

"Please don't tell Buddy I called you, but I want you to help me. He doesn't know I'm calling you. You have connections, Bob, I know *The New York Times* has connections."

I figured out what she was trying to say:

She wanted *me* to help her get a job.

She hadn't lost her looks, she continued, and had never had cosmetic surgery.

"I'm getting ready to go back to work, you know," she said. "I'm looking for something. But it won't be a role for an old lady. I don't look like an old lady, and I don't feel like it."

The 82 year old octogenarian, once the most famous actress in the world, asked me to contact a producer, director or others in Hollywood and let them know she was available and ready to work and to ask what parts she'd be suitable for. She didn't seem to doubt she could get any part she wanted.

I was befuddled and felt awkward. Not knowing what else to say, I promised I'd see what I could do.

A couple of evenings later she called again. Her voice full of anxiety. "Have you heard anything, Bob?"

I was getting in deeper and deeper and, not wanting to hurt her, I lied and said I'd called around and learned the studios were having a tough time of it lately and not making as many movies.

"I know that," she said, and then added she thought too many movies were "trashy," implying they contained too much sex, and adding audiences were being turned off by "all those people taking off their clothes."

She seemed to understand film production was in the doldrums but called four more times during the next few days, always proclaiming how much she was looking forward to starring in another movie while trying to convince me to continue keeping an eye out for roles she'd like.

I wondered if she was lonely or depressed, but Mary always insisted she was happy and loved to gossip with me One day she said she was so excited about the Oscars that she was planning to buy a new dress. Another day she'd had a visit from her best friend, actress Lillian Gish; another day she'd taken a pleasant drive along the beach with Buddy.

She often spoke as if as Hollywood still made silent films and reminisced about Chaplin, Clara Bow, Joan Crawford, D.W. Griffith and long gone silent screen stars as if they were still alive.

If I ever came close to asking about Douglas Fairbanks, she turned the conversation to another subject.

A few days before the Oscars, I spoke to her for the last time. She was "overwhelmed" by the upcoming event, she said, although Buddy had vetoed her attending the ceremony as "too much for me" and the Academy was going to deliver her statute to Pickfair.

I went to Pickfair only one more time, about a year later, a fund raiser for a charity I don't remember. Buddy Rogers greeted me, along with Sandy, like an old friend and apologized that Mary wasn't feeling well so I wouldn't be able to talk to her that evening.

My last vision of Pickfair was looking across its vast living room that night and seeing Lillian Gish sitting alone on a sofa staring into the distance while a huge portrait of Mary, long blonde curls circling a pretty face, looked down on her.

Mary died two years later in 1979, Buddy died in 1999.

By then Pickfair had been sold to the owner of the Los Angeles Lakers, then resold, then finally torn down by a movie mogul who replaced it with a huge Tuscan villa, and Pickfair was gone.

18

A week or so after my first visit to Pickfair, I discovered one of the perks of being the Los Angeles Bureau Chief of *The Times*--an annual invitation to the Oscar ceremony hand delivered to my home. Sandy selected a beautiful Japanese silk gown she kept in reserve for special occasions, and I sent my tuxedo to the cleaners. After we arrived at the Dorothy Chandler Pavilion and walked down the red carpet, drawing stares from fans who had no idea who we were, we were ushered to fourth row seats left of center stage.

We sat down and looked around trying to look casual while searching for celebrities seated near us. Then it occurred to me: how was I going to cover the Academy Awards from the audience? How do I call in my story to New York? I found a pay phone (no cell phones yet) in the lobby but it would be difficult going back and forth to report the awarding of each Oscar.

Only later did I realize reporters never covered the Oscars from the audience. The hundreds of journalists credentialed to cover the awards were herded into a room far from the stage and watched the proceedings on television. Then the winners, gripping their new Oscars, were paraded before them and answered the shouted questions of a hundred voices.

"I'll be back," I told Sandy and bounded up the stairs on the left side of the stage and tried to disappear behind a curtain, expecting someone to stop me or ask me what I was doing there. Nobody did. It was about 40 minutes before curtain time, and stagehands and crews from the ABC television network in black tie were making final preparations for its broadcast. I tried to blend in with them and spotted a clipboard atop a stack of cables snaking across the floor backstage. I lifted it up, hugged it to my chest and elected to stay, hoping to blend into the crowd of tuxedo-clad technicians and that the clipboard would be a sort of badge enabling me to be there.

As a hiding place I chose a dark area behind the safety curtain located near the back of the huge stage. When the orchestra opened with a medley of movie music, I moved closer to the main event, to just off the left wing of the stage, holding the clipboard establishing my right to be there.

Nobody inquired who I was, and as the Oscar winners left the stage after collecting their trophies I was waiting in the wings to greet them.

The biggest winner that night was *"One Flew Over the Cuckoo's Nest,"* honored with awards for best picture, best director, best actor and best actress, the first time a movie had made such a sweep since *"It Happened One Night"* in 1934.

"Jesus, I'm shaken up," Jack Nicholson, best actor winner for *"Cuckoo's Nest,"* told me a second after leaving the stage Oscar in hand. I introduced myself as a reporter for *The New York Times.* He didn't seem surprised by my lurking in the wings and did a quick dance as he answered me:

"I'd hoped, but we got about half way through and we hadn't won anything and it didn't look so good. Then Milos (Director Milos Forman) won and it started looking better. I'm really shaken."

One by one, as winners and presenters walked off the stage I waited with my clipboard and questions: George Burns, who won a supporting actor trophy for "Sunshine Boys" along with a standing ovation, and answered me simply, "I'm thrilled."

Louise Fletcher, "Nurse Ratchett" in "Cuckoo's Nest" looked at me as if I was a certified idiot when I asked how the award made her feel seconds after she left the stage.

"Are you kidding? What do *you* think?"

It was getting close to my 11 o'clock deadline and I needed to call New York. A former war correspondent once told me that, however good your story is, it's no good unless you can't get it to your editors by your deadline, so the first thing you do is establish a dependable communication link. During an earlier reconnaissance back stage, I'd spotted a telephone on the floor apparently meant for the use of ABC staffers and hoped it would be available when I needed it.

A dark haired, beautiful woman passed a couple of feet from me toward the stage. Our eyes met and Elizabeth Taylor responded with a smile. I heard her name being announced as she continued toward center stage to reveal the "best picture" winner (*"Cuckoo's Nest"*).

I stepped across the rivers of cables, found the telephone unused and dialed the *Times*. As I waited for the New York Dictation Room to come on line, the floor beneath me started shaking.

In full force, the University of Southern California marching band was striding on to the stage. As I hid behind a curtain, Elizabeth Taylor led the audience singing "America the Beautiful," almost drowning out my voice as I dictated my story to the recording room in New York. I out shouted her and the band and made my deadline.

19

On a Sunday in January a few months later, the weekend National Desk editor told me to check out a wire service report two Californians had been arrested as Russian spies--one in Mexico City, the other near the campus of the University of California in Riverside east of Los Angeles. I reported their arrests, a front page story, and several months later covered the Federal Court trials of Andrew Daulton Lee, the small time drug dealer arrested outside the Soviet Embassy in Mexico City, and Christopher John Boyce, his childhood friend whom the FBI said had held a classified position at one of Southern California's largest government contractors, TRW Systems Inc., before enrolling at U.C. Riverside.

Boyce was 23, Lee, 22. Both were from the Palos Verdes Peninsula, a rocky outcropping about 25 miles west of downtown Los Angeles where most of the expensive homes overlooking the Pacific were required to have red tile roofs, complying with the original developers' goal of simulating a village on the Mediterranean. As it happened, it's where I lived.

Boyce was tried first. On the opening day, prosecutors claimed that while working as a communications clerk linking TRW to CIA headquarters in Virginia, Australia and elsewhere, Boyce stole thousands of *Top Secret* documents--often taking them home in potted plants-- and passed them to Lee, who flew to Mexico City or Vienna and sold them to KGB agents. Lee in turn took the Russians' money and bought drugs to sell in Southern California.

A college dropout, Boyce got his $140 a week job in the CIA communications vault (called the "Black Vault" because of its role in secret intelligence) through his father, a former FBI agent and chief of security at another local defense plant.

The prosecutors' opening argument was curiously vague. But largely because of my experience writing about Lockheed's spy satellites in Sunnyvale, I realized beneath their fuzzy allegations was a huge story: Boyce and Lee were accused of compromising one of America's most secret intelligence gathering systems, which used satellites lurking at 22,000 miles in space to scoop up Soviet radio and radar traffic and eavesdrop on ICBM tests, a system crucial to monitoring any arms control agreements being negotiated with the USSR.

As the trial progressed, during recesses I got to know the defendants' mothers, siblings and lawyers, even their parish priest, and was fascinated by the question: why did two young men from one of the most affluent communities in America sell out their country?

Boyce's lawyers mounted a defense asserting the information sold in Mexico City was outdated and therefore useless to the Russians; Lee's lawyers claimed the CIA set up the pair to spread "disinformation" to the Russians. But the lawyers had little to work with and Boyce and Lee (at separate trials), were convicted. Boyce was sentenced to 40 years in prison, Lee, because of his previous record of arrests, got life. Robert Kelleher, the Federal judge who presided, said he regretted that prevailing Federal law prevented him from ordering the death penalty because of the serious damage done to national security by the two friends.

After his conviction Boyce's lawyers invited me to interview him at a Federal prison in San Pedro a few miles from Palos Verdes. I found him likeable, smart and articulate with an air of youthful innocence and idealism. I proposed an article on the case to the editor of the *Times Sunday Magazine* and it was published under the headline *"To Be Young, Rich and a Spy."* At his trial and the interview Boyce claimed he hadn't intended to become a spy but while at work in the

Black Vault had learned the United States was betraying its ally Australia by not sharing intelligence information as required by treaty and was interfering in Australian domestic labor affairs in order to keep the secret Pine Gap satellite receiving station in the Outback that I'd written about for the *Mercury-News* in operation. He claimed that after so many senseless deaths in Vietnam and government lies justifying the war, he was disgusted with his country and asked his friend, Daulton Lee, to help publicize the betrayal by taking the information to a reporter.

Instead, he claimed Daulton took the classified documents he copied to the Soviet Embassy in Mexico and sold them to the KGB, and after that Boyce claimed he had no choice but to continue giving secret documents to Lee because he threatened blackmail if he didn't. I never believed this implausible story, nor did his jury. Lee's motives were clear: he liked the money. Boyce's motives, I thought, were a blend of idealism rooted in his criticism of purported U.S. misdeeds, an appetite for adventure and risk taking, a contempt for authority and not incidentally, money. (The exact amount was never disclosed-- in all, the Russians appeared to have paid them at least $100,000) I suspected he initially made an impulsive offer to Lee to sell the secrets in Mexico, then as months passed and Lee pressed him for more secrets to finance his drug business, he realized the depth of the grave he had dug himself into, quit his job at TRW and enrolled in college, too late to head off the consequences of what he'd done.

After *To Be Young, Rich and A Spy* ran in the Sunday *Times*, Jonathan Coleman, a youthful editor at the New York publisher Simon & Schuster (and later bestselling author), asked if I was interested in writing a book based on the article. I accepted his offer, not realizing how difficult it would be to produce a book while having to get on an airliner every few days to cover a story for *The Times* somewhere in the West.

For the next year and a half every weekend and vacation day was spent at my typewriter (we still used typewriters in 1977-79) or interviewing people involved in the story. With encouragement from Coleman, I decided to attempt what some writers call a "non fiction novel," also sometimes called "narrative non-fiction." The best known example may be Truman Capote's *In Cold Blood,* his account of the senseless murder of a family in Kansas, although a bigger influence on me was *Blood and Money* by Thomas Thompson, a fast paced account of a murder in Houston. Writing a "non fiction novel" is an attempt to create the illusion of a novel using real characters and events to weave a narrative the author hopes is as compelling as a work of fiction; it takes a lot of work and research: interviewing in great detail as many of the characters involved in the story as possible, confirming their stories, finding as many significant documents involving the case as you can, comparing multiple, often contradictory accounts of the same events. Some details needed to replicate a coherent novel may not be available; some people may refuse to talk to an author or will lie or demand money for whatever information they have, lying if it brings in more money. The gravest transgression of a "nonfiction novelist" is *inventing* dialogue or events, which I'm convinced I've observed in some non-fiction novels. Fortunately, Boyce and Lee's lawyers generously allowed me to copy thousands of documents, many classified Top Secret, that the government was required to give them for mounting the defense, as well as their notes and diaries on the case. Boyce encouraged me to write the book. Virtually every night I accepted a collect call (paid for incidentally by *The Times*) from him at the Federal penitentiary at Lompoc, California northwest of Santa Barbara, and I interviewed him about his life and the espionage; he wrote me more than twenty letters--many beautifully written that I quoted verbatim in the book.

I interviewed him face to face several times at the prison and twice spoke to Lee at the same prison, although he refused to say much unless I paid him "a lot of money." As a result of his resistance and Boyce's eager cooperation, the book tells the story more from Boyce's point of view than Lee's. (During one visit, in a note trying to convince me he was the victim of a "C.I.A. disinformation operation" Lee referred to himself as "a snowman," I asked what that meant; "Cocaine dealer," he said. Lee told his lawyer that when a Soviet agent needed a code name for Boyce someone chose "Falcon," a reference to a longtime hobby of falconry).

While I worked on the book, there was still lots of news to cover for *The Times*: the 1978 passage of Proposition 13 and the earth-moving California tax revolt that led to it…a financial scandal in Hollywood… the mass suicide in Guyana of more than 900 members of San Francisco's People's Temple …the run up to the 1984 Olympics in Los Angeles and much more, hundreds of stories. A couple of years earlier I'd spent a lot of time in Phoenix reporting about the assassination of Don Bolles, a reporter for the *Arizona Republic*, after he'd written stories embarrassing to a wealthy rancher and liquor distributor. In 1979 a reporter for a weekly newspaper whom I'd met during these visits to Phoenix called and said if I'd fly to Arizona he'd tell me a story that would make my trip worth it.

It was this call that led to my kidnapping by Cesar Chavez. ("Kidnapping" is probably an overstatement, but that's how I remember it).

Chavez was the charismatic migrant farm worker who beginning in the early seventies achieved near mythic status as the venerated cofounder of the United Farm Workers, leading a David vs. Goliath battle against California fruit and vegetable growers. The press, including The *New York Times*, jumped on the story of this seemingly modest, non-violent Latino taking on forces of evil, comparing his battle with those of exploited Dust Bowl refugees portrayed in John Steinbeck's *"Grapes of Wrath."* It was an image Chavez at first acquired spontaneously, then cultivated by presenting himself as an iconic reincarnation of Mohandas K. Ghandi or Martin Luther King selflessly leading a non violent campaign to gain liberty and fairness for the exploited. Robert F. Kennedy marched with Chavez, as did thousands of other sympathizers; perhaps millions more stopped buying table grapes from California because of a boycott proclaimed by Chavez.

When I got to Phoenix my friend claimed there was a flip side to Chavez that reporters had missed. He introduced me to farm workers from Texas and Arizona who claimed they had been attempting for over a year to organize a farm workers' union that was not dominated by Chavez but he had blocked them at every turn, warning them against creating a union not under his control and sabotaging their appeals for financial support to government agencies, private foundations and other organizations; then they introduced me to former U.F.W. organizers, former allies of Chavez, who corroborated most of what the others said. They claimed Chavez had become a paranoid, domineering megalomaniac allied with a man named Chuck Dederich, founder of the Synanon drug rehabilitation group, and applied Dederich's management style of viciously and verbally abusing his lieutenants in a ritual called "The Game."

They said he tolerated no dissent and insensitively purged from his organization several loyal Jewish liberals who had been among his earliest supporters and strategists. Worse, they said that during a strike in Arizona's melon fields in the mid- 1970s, the strike leader, Chavez' closest friend and cousin, had organized a violent U.F.W. campaign against potential strike breakers never publicized in the United States by establishing what they called a 100 mile wide "wet line" (as in "wetback") at the border. Job hunting newcomers from Mexico, I was told, were met at the border and beaten by U.F.W.- recruited thugs with clubs, chains and barbed wire whips to discourage them from taking striking workers' jobs in the U.S. fields; when that didn't't work, there were bombings in Mexican border towns that destroyed homes and cars.

So much for the gentle non violent darling of liberals. It was not a project I enjoyed undertaking. Like a lot of people I'd swallowed the legend of the non violent farm worker who battled the exploitive barons of agriculture. It fit my liberal biases. But once I heard the allegations it was impossible ethically to ignore them. That's the way it has to be with reporters. Once you're told a story like that that may be true, you have no choice but to follow it up wherever it leads you.

20

I spent almost two weeks in Arizona, Texas and along the California-Mexico border confirming what I'd been told. Border town policemen and others corroborated the story. I hired a Spanish speaker to translate Mexican newspaper reports and interviewing witnesses confirming the Wet Line violence had occurred and who was behind it. But before I could write anything I had to approach Chavez and ask him to respond to the allegations.

I knew it wouldn't be pleasant. At the time, he was leading another strike along an arid stretch of the Imperial Valley made unnaturally lush by water channeled from the Colorado Rockies hundreds of miles away. I called his public relations manager and asked for a brief interview with Chavez in El Centro, the border town that was the economic center of the region and the site of the strike; two days later, expecting, I think, for me to write another chapter in the heroic David vs. Goliath saga, he set up an early evening appointment with Chavez at my hotel in El Centro.

About an hour after the interview was scheduled, the P.R. rep called my room and asked me to meet him in the lobby. He was waiting for me with five large Latino men, who I later realized were Chavez' bodyguards.

"Where's your car?," he asked.

I pointed to it.

"Give him your keys," he said, referring to one of the bodyguards.

Not understanding what was happening, I gave him my car keys, then the other men herded me into a car waiting outside.

Chavez was in the back seat.

We drove off at high speed with me sandwiched between Chavez and a bodyguard and another bodyguard in the front passenger seat. "Where are we going?" I asked.

Chavez said we were driving to the United Farm Workers headquarters in the San Joaquin Valley town of Keene where Chavez lived--*almost three hundred miles away.*

"Where's my car?

"It'll be all right," he said. "Your car's behind us."

I asked him to stop and said I couldn't leave El Centro because my typewriter and suitcase were in my hotel room.

Chavez ignored me and we continued through the darkness. With his goons surrounding me, I was going to have to ask him some *very embarrassing* questions.

I started in: I told him what I'd been told about the UFW violence and the "wet line," the car bombings, the purge of his early Jewish advisors, his introduction of "The Game"

Chavez, I realized, was not used to having a reporter write anything that wasn't hagiography.

"What's going on?," he asked. "Somebody's trying to do a number on me."

Yes, he conceded, "we had a 'wet line.' it cost us a lot of money, and we stopped a lot of illegals." But he asserted he didn't know anything about violence during the strike.

I showed him photocopied Spanish language stories from border town newspapers reporting the house and car bombings.

"If it happened, I know nothing about it. I tried to look into it. I talked to all of the Mexican officials I could get hold of; I checked everybody to get a feeling of what had happened, but I didn't find anything that made me feel anything wrong had happened."

The bodyguard next to me glared.

As if checking off items on a shopping list, I continued to ask my questions one by one, meanwhile wondering, "Where are we and where's my car?"

After another half hour of requests to let me out of his car, Chavez instructed his driver to stop, which he did, in the middle of nowhere. He didn't say anything as I left.

As I got out of the car, I saw my leased *Times'* Chevrolet idling on the shoulder of the desert highway. I happily drove back to El Centro, thankful there was enough gas in the tank to get me there, and I went to bed. The story ran two days later. From then on, whenever I turned up at a United Farm Workers rally I was shadowed wherever I went by a menacing gang of goons.

21

     Abe Rosenthal called from New York to say he was flying to California for several days and told me to arrange delivery of the *Times* at his hotel at a desert resort outside Palm Springs. After calling around I learned delivery wasn't available at the resort and told him.

     "Get the paper to me, whatever you have to do." By the day he arrived, I'd arranged to have two copies of the paper placed on a Los

Angeles commuter flight to Palm Springs each morning from where--at the *Times'* expense-- a taxi delivered them to his hotel.

Abe at 58 was a chunky, jowly man with dark hair and dark rimmed eyeglasses that gave him an owlish look of constant curiosity. He favored bowties, enhancing his professorial look. He had recently completed his ascendancy to the top editorial post at the paper--Executive Editor--after a long and perhaps inevitable rise for a smart, driven, talented, ambitious journalist, his triumph even more impressive because he was the first executive editor who was Jewish. (For more than a century the Ochs-Sulzberger family which owned the paper had avoided appointing a top editor who was Jewish to avoid strengthening the hand of *Times* bashers who considered it "a Jewish newspaper.") Born in 1922 in Sault Ste. Marie, Ontario, Canada, into a working class family that emigrated to the Bronx in the 1930's, Abe was sickly as a child, a victim of osteomyelitis, a bone marrow disease, but prevailed over chronic pain and multiple hospitalizations to attend the City College of New York, a workingman's institution with impressive academic standards that for more than a century had nurtured ambitious, often first and second generation Jews. He landed a job as the *Times'* campus correspondent in 1943 and a year later was offered a full time job and before long was a distinguished foreign correspondent, Pulitzer Prize winner, then an editor who became something of an heroic figure in journalism for defying the Nixon Administration and pressing to publish the Pentagon Papers. Among many reporters and junior editors at *The New York Times* he had a reputation as thin skinned and domineering , a tyrant with a long memory who took the slightest difference of opinion as an affront that could ruin careers at the *Times.* In my view he improved a very good newspaper by inducing a culture of integrity rooted in a climate of fear; he stressed accuracy, fairness and absence of bias but because of his personality quirks lot of good reporters and editors ran afoul of him, often unjustly. His goal, he said, was "to keep the paper straight." He thought of himself as the "conscience" of the institution and when it made an error or missed an important story, he took it personally. Despite the *Times'* reputation for liberal bias, he was impatient with liberal clichés and called himself "a bleeding heart conservative." Together with his friend, Arthur Gelb, he may have saved the *Times* from extinction-- during a period when New York City was facing huge economic problems--by redesigning the paper, creating new special sections with better writing, more features and a palate of coverage aimed at appealing to a national audience of educated, affluent readers, allowing it to grow nationally despite the city's financial problems. (I was as afraid of him as anyone, but never landed in his doghouse, even after refusing assignments to Teheran and El Salvador where he wanted to send me. To be candid, I became one of his fair haired boys, deservedly or not.)

Although I don't think Abe ever thanked me for my feat in arranging delivery of the paper in Palm Springs, he called the L.A. Bureau from there and said "we" would be driving to L.A. the next day and he wanted to have dinner with Sandy and me. For a correspondent at a bureau far from the home office, a visit by the Executive Editor was a monumentally big deal Other than the day he was among the eight editors who interviewed me for a job and the day he let me know I'd passed my probation, I'd never spoken to him. When he asked us for dinner, I assumed we'd meet his wife, Ann Marie, who'd he'd met and married when he was a young reporter covering the United Nations.

The following evening, Sandy and I met the woman he brought with him, Katherine Balfour, beginning a long, secret and ultimately troubled relationship with her.

When Katherine was about 26 more than thirty years before, she had earned stunning reviews as Alma, the central figure in the original cast of Tennessee Williams' play *Summer and Smoke* and followed this success with a succession of roles on Broadway, television and the movies, playing, for example, the mother of Ryan O'Neal's Oliver Barrett in the saccharine blockbuster *Love Story*.

A daughter of Jewish immigrants from Eastern Europe, she was 59 when we met and still a beauty, with long dark hair and full, dark eyes. She had been Abe's mistress for almost fifteen years, a secret he had kept from his colleagues at the paper.

After her early successes as an actress she never became the marquee star she wanted to be, she said, and blamed it on her long affair with Abe:

She had to be ready at any moment, she said, to travel to meet him for a secret tryst in the United States or abroad. As a result, she told Sandy and me, she had not been able to keep her promising career on track. Now, she said, she intended to make a comeback.

Even before Katherine told us this story during our dinner at the Bistro Garden in Beverly Hills it was obvious the two of them were romantically connected. Abe didn't try to hide it. As far as I knew, none of my friends at *The Times* knew anything about Abe's mistress despite the hyperactive internal gossip mill that flourished among obsessively curious, insecure professional information-gatherers at The *Times*. This was top secret information that I intended to keep quiet, information I didn't dare spread because of Abe's reputation for ruining a reporter's career if you crossed him.

That dinner was the first of many get togethers of the four of us in California and New York. As was customary for the Bureau Chief when the boss came to town, I picked up the tab--and put it on my NYT expense account, although he signed the bill at most of our subsequent dinners.

Because she planned to resume her acting career Katherine told us that first night that she'd be spending more time in California and looked forward to seeing us again. Katherine seemed to bond enthusiastically with Sandy that evening as if she had found her new best friend.

Abe, meanwhile, seemed supportive of her dream of revitalizing her career, and Sandy and I said we would be anxious to see her on her next visit, not realizing it would be to our home.

22

After nearly a year researching and writing *The Falcon and the Snowman* (rewriting parts of it three times) I sent the manuscript to Simon & Schuster, glad to be done with it, unable to look at it without wanting to throw up. I was sick of it.

Chris Boyce called nightly and I updated him on the preparations leading up to publication, in which he was very interested. I had become fond of him and even encouraged my daughter, Susan, to write him in prison. As publication day approached, Chris tipped me about a plot by the spies' lawyers to make an end run around plans to make a movie out of *Falcon*. Separately, two different schlocky producers had promised the lawyers a big payday if they persuaded their clients to sign over rights to their life stories without buying rights to my book--not unusual in the back stabbing, mendacious Hollywood culture. In early December, 1979 at his suggestion, I made the four hour drive to Lompoc and Chris signed papers assigning exclusive rights to his life story to me, foreclosing the scam. I thanked him and asked if there was anything he needed for Christmas.

"I could use some new running shoes," he said, and I sent him a pair of Etonic sports shoes as a Christmas gift.

Less than a month later, Chris persuaded his keepers to assign him to the prison landscape crew. Several days later he fashioned a dummy out of prison waste, laid it on his bunk and covered it with a blanket--producing the illusion of a sleeping inmate that Clint Eastwood created in the movie *Escape from Alcatraz,* which had recently been shown at the penitentiary.

When other members of the grounds crew returned to their cells, Chris lingered, lifted a steel grate covering a drainage basin that he had made deeper over several days of clandestine digging and lowered himself into the ground as if dropping into a grave. He waited for darkness, which arrived early in January, then pulled himself out of the drainage basin, scaled two razor wire topped fences using a makeshift ladder he'd hidden, and was gone, running as fast as he could in his new running shoes.

23

The Falcon and the Snowman was published in October, 1979. For a first- time author it couldn't have been more enjoyable: favourable reviews, serialization in *LIFE* magazine, a Book of the Month selection, sales to publishers in almost a dozen countries, full-page ads in *The Times*, a paperback sale, a successful auction of the movie rights, a national book tour.

I missed some of the initial hoopla because I was traveling the country in a jetliner chartered by Ronald Reagan's presidential campaign. Each Monday morning about 8 am Ronald and Nancy Reagan, their staff and a contingent of reporters took off from a corporate jet terminal at Los Angeles International Airport and took us to campaign battlegrounds around the country, often four or five states in a day, with Reagan giving an almost identical stump speech at each stop. From the reaction of his audiences it was soon obvious that Reagan, with his amiable personality and persuasive demands for less government and a stronger military, was touching a chord with his audiences.

Usually we returned to L.A. Friday night too late for dinner with Sandy. Besides disrupting my home life it wasn't the kind of reporting I enjoyed. Every morning, reporters got out of bed with one purpose in mind: to get Reagan to make a gaffe that gave them a story for the day, and then they could relax. It was "gotcha" journalism---probably a result of the Watergate era's lionization of "investigative reporters" Woodward and Bernstein. In my opinion, "gotcha journalism" discouraged deeper coverage of the presidential race although I confess I joined the hunt one day. After two months or so listening to him on the campaign trail I thought I understood how Reagan felt on most issues--he was essentially a libertarian, opposed to government dictates and in favor of individual choice and liberty-- and so at a meeting with reporters at Jacksonville, Florida I set him up with a question whose answer I was certain I knew.

In earlier campaign appearances he'd suggested that the U.S. should establish a military presence in Pakistan to demonstrate American disapproval of the Soviet invasion of its neighbor, Afghanistan. Separately, there was growing international concern at the time over the spread of nuclear weapons, especially among rival regional powers such as India and Pakistan, and I asked him if he'd accept in principle Pakistan developing a nuclear weapon if that was its price for hosting U.S. troops near Afghanistan.

"Yes," he said emphatically. "I just don't think it's any of our business."

Reagan seemed to be saying that he would not attempt as President to halt the spread of nuclear weapons. Within an hour, his staff, alarmed by his comments, summoned reporters to an impromptu, unscheduled meeting where he backed off on his earlier remarks: in fact he said he *supported* American efforts to stop the proliferation of nuclear weapons, then added he doubted it could be successful, bringing a collective grimace from his advisors. Jimmy Carter's campaign staff aired a TV commercial the following day with film of our exchange, claiming that Reagan as president wouldn't try to stem the spread of atomic weapons, but the campaign moved on the following day, and it probably had no effect on the election.

(Another confession: despite a few doubts about Reagan, I switched my registration from Democrat to Republican so I could vote for him. After college I'd been a typical run of the mill liberal, but while working for the *San Jose Mercury-News* I'd written a series of articles about Lyndon Johnson's Great Society programs that taught me how much money could be wasted by some programs championed by liberals: one Jobs Corps training camp I wrote about spent $25,000 a year to teach each trainee an entry level skill, substantially more than a year at Harvard. At least for awhile I became disenchanted with the liberals' view Federal cash could solve any problem. But as soon as George W. Bush was elected and launched his catastrophic invasion of Iraq, I promptly and enthusiastically became a registered Democrat again.)

Although many fought for assignments to the presidential campaign as a career enhancer (if the candidate you covered won it often meant a prestigious White House assignment), I wasn't interested in moving to Washington, and after four months of protests I convinced editors to let me return to my regular beat in California.

Because of the publicity over *Falcon* I began getting calls from friends I hadn't heard from in decades, including a lot of the classmates who had shunned and scorned me as a duck-tailed piece of Trailer Trash.

At an Inglewood High School reunion, when a dozen former classmates lined up to ask for my autograph, my satisfaction was complete.

It wasn't only former high school classmates who wanted to look me up. Members of the family that owned *The Times*, including Iphigene Sulzberger, its elderly matriarch, invited Sandy and me to dinner to discuss the book during a visit to L.A.

My high school journalism teacher, Bill Kamrath, sent me a letter he'd written to all his former students headlined "A Confession" praising *Falcon* enthusiastically and apologizing for underestimating my journalistic skills when I was at Inglewood High. (He didn't mention firing me as co editor of the paper after the print shop cherry bomb exploded.).

Letters started to arrive whose only return address was the name and a number. They were from convicts around the country who had read the book and claimed they had better stories to tell and would tell them to me if I shared my book royalties with them.

Several letters came from a man named Byron De La Beckwith Jr. Because I was named Lindsey, the maiden name as his wife, an omen, they had decided I should write his autobiography, and in return they promised me six acres of land they owned in Signal Mountain, Tennessee.

Of course I recognized his name:. Beckwith was the Ku Klux Klansman who had long been the prime suspect in the 1963 murder of civil rights activist Medgar Evers. Twice he'd been tried for murder but both trials ended in hung juries—juries stacked with Mississippi white supremacists and sympathizers

I had high hopes: Perhaps, if I played my cards right, I could get him to confess to the murder. I wrote back and said I was eager to take on the job. He sent me pages and pages filled with ugly racist rantings and justifications why the South was biblically entitled to continue segregation. Both he and his wife seemed to me to be nuts, but our correspondence continued for months as I kept urging him sympathetically to tell me the truth about Evers' death and I waxed enthusiastically about living on Signal Mountain. But I guess he was savvy enough to realize what I was trying to do and refused to comment about Evers; after several months I wrote a letter telling them I had taken on another book project and couldn't write his life story.

Eventually Federal prosecutors went after him. He was arrested at his new home in Signal Mountain, Tennessee—on the property he'd offered me. In 1994 he was convinced of murder and sentenced to life in prison; he died there in 2001.

After *Falcon* was published I learned how "experts" are sometimes created in America: Suddenly I was being called by one news organization after another asking me to analyze the latest case of espionage even though it had nothing to do with the case I'd written about.

CNN, NBC and a German television network sent correspondents to interview me; National Public Radio called often for my views on the latest of a spy. All I'd done was write about a single case of espionage and was asked to pontificate about espionage cases reaching back to World War II. The saddest part of the experience was that not only did I respond, I played the part. Responding as their "expert" and knowingly pontificating with my views about the ancient art of espionage.

It was all very flattering, too much so. I was getting a big head, which was not good for a journalist--something you're not supposed to do. I'm afraid it would get worse. And I'd come to realize I'd broken another cardinal rule of journalists: Don't get close to a person you write about.

24

About ten o'clock one evening in October, 1980, the telephone rang at our home in Palos Verdes and I heard coins dropping into a pay telephone box, then the voice of Christopher Boyce.

Without telling me where he was, he said he'd wanted me to tell his parents he was alive and in good health and he loved them.

That week the U.S. Marshals Service, frustrated and embarrassed by its unsuccessful ten month search for Boyce, had established a special task force in Los Angeles to find him with a budget of nearly a million dollars.

Chris asked whether his escape from prison had boosted sales of *The Falcon and the Snowman*, and I said it had.

"Good!," he said.

The call was brief. Before it ended, I said:

"I'm going to have to tell them you called."

"Do what you have to do."

Although some reporters had speculated the CIA or KGB helped him escape, Chris said he'd done it on his own, using the Clint

Eastwood ruse portrayed in *Escape from Alcatraz*. Still, as he scaled the two high fences using the makeshift ladder he said, "My knees were shaking. I thought I was going to get a bullet in my head." Once he was over the two fences he said he'd hidden in the countryside north of the prison, then, with help of friends he'd made in prison, managed to evade his pursuers and start a new life.

"I could see the lights at night and the helicopters looking for me. His last words to me were:

"I've never felt better. I love being free."

First I called the National Desk, then his mother, then the Marshals Service command post. Members of the task force later told me the phone call confirming he was alive re-energized their search, which by then had extended fruitlessly to South Africa, Australia and Costa Rica.

A reporter for *People* magazine wrote a profile of me that in retrospect shows how far I'd gone over the line journalistically:

" Boyce's dramatic flight came just as the Lindsey book became a best seller and made the author a minor celebrity." There was no question that he was a spy," he said, but "he was the kind of person I would admire as a friend. I saw Chris as a very nice, sensitive kid who made a mistake when he was 21.. Despite what he did, and I don't minimize it for a minute, he has many fine qualities. I couldn't ever find anyone who said a negative thing about him. He's a man of high principles. [Boy, did I regret that later.] I was getting very close to him and that really is very bad for a reporter to do. Chris became like a member of my family."

25

One of the realities of being the Los Angeles Bureau Chief of *The New York Times* is that people are nice to you whether they like you or not. *The Times* has a broad reach and many people and organizations want to disseminate their opinions or accomplishments via its pages. In L.A., not only do actors, directors and press agents vie for attention in the Newspaper of Record, many producers, studio executives and agents are relocated New Yorkers, and a mention in the newspaper they grew up reading seems to help them validate their success.

As soon as Sandy and I landed in Los Angeles our mailbox was filled with invitations: to parties at producers' Beverly Hills homes, banquets, movie premieres, openings of new boutiques on Rodeo Drive, award ceremonies (the Oscars, Grammies, Emmys, etc., even a party to celebrate a new brand of tequila. (That invitation came from Bing Crosby, an investor in the Mexican distiller. Who could turn *him* down? Even John Wayne and Cary Grant arrived to sample the new tequila that night.)

There was an uproar among Beverly Hills residents over goings on at a multi-million dollar mansion on Sunset Boulevard that was the locale for one of the more bizarre parties we attended. The 38 room home had been bought by an oil rich Saudi Arabian sheik for his 22 year old son and the son's 19 year old bride, and the couple had spent millions remodeling the white, sprawling 61 year old mansion, painting it lime green and topping its long fence along Sunset Boulevard with marble statues of copulating couples and nude women with realistic skin tones, including pubic hair.

News reports attracted sightseers and touched off 24 hour a day bumper to bumper traffic jams (and not a few collisions) on Sunset. Saying he wanted to be a good neighbor, the sheik invited neighbors, film stars and local politicians to a party at the house. There were two bands, three bars and three long buffet tables featuring 30 pounds of iced Iranian caviar, more than 200 two-pound Maine lobsters and much more. As his guests pounced on the bountiful buffet, Sheik Mohammed al-Fassi (his son and his wife were absent) offered to give me, Sandy, the mayor of Beverly Hills and another reporter a tour of the house.

It was an experience to be remembered. Some rooms were seemingly transplanted from an Arabian Nights fantasy, draped with sheets of red and yellow embroidered, gold veined fabric that created the illusion of living in a tent at a desert oasis; the master bedroom had a revolving circular bed with a mirror on the ceiling; costly French impressionist paintings hung next to black velvet paintings of veiled, nude women and the bride's high school diploma.

In the basement was a disco outfitted, the sheik said, at a cost of $100,000. If one word could describe the décor, it was tasteless.

In the end, the community's curiosity --and appetite for expensive food--sated, Beverly Hills officials welcomed the sheik's son and his wife to the city. Unfortunately, they soon divorced and never returned to the house, and according to news reports, the caterer who supplied the caviar and lobsters filed suit claiming he hadn't been paid.

Not long after the sheik's party, Sandy and I were invited to dinner at the Santa Monica home of Gordon Davidson, the well regarded director of the Center Theater Group in downtown Los Angeles and his equally well regarded wife, Judi, a publicist who undoubtedly wanted to strengthen relations with *The New York Times*.

When we arrived, four tables, each for six diners, were set up in the dining and living rooms of the two story home. We were among the first to arrive and Judi poured us glasses of wine. Within a few minutes a tall, lanky fellow with dark hair and a pretty blonde woman beside him shambled into the room. Walter Matthau extended a friendly hand and said: "I've given up introducing myself by name."

Once all the guests had arrived Judi led us to our seats. To stimulate conversation, she said she always assigned couples to different tables at dinner parties. Sandy joined a table with several members of the cast of the epic TV miniseries, "*Roots*," which made it difficult for her; we hadn't watched it.

At my table, the actor Hal Holbrook, a self-assured, unfriendly sort, sat on one side of me, and on the other was Matthau's blonde wife, Carol.

I had just completed *"The Falcon and the Snowman"* and mentioned it, and Carol and I spent the dinner talking, mostly about spies. She said she was interested in anything regarding espionage because she thought her stepfather (whom she obviously adored) did some kind of secret work for the British Secret Intelligence Service, MI6, during World War II although he'd never been able to discuss it with her.

She also seemed to be obsessed with a German spymaster who had been hanged on the orders of Hitler in 1945.

26

Despite wanting to share my secret of Abe's long-running affair--a sure hit on the NYT's competitive gossip mill and I was as much of a gossip as anyone else-- I still kept quiet. If I'd spoken up and he'd found out, my next assignment would have been in Outer Mongolia. When Katherine called to say she was coming to L.A for an audition and needed a place to stay, Sandy and I felt we had to offer her the bedroom in our house vacated after Susan's departure for college, although we didn't really expect her to take us up on it. We warned her it that it was at least an hour's drive from Palos Verdes to any of the film studios. We didn't realize she expected us to drive her to the auditions.

She camped out in Susan's room repeatedly during the next three or four years while expecting Sandy (or me if I was available) to deliver her to her audition or, in one case, to the Beverly Hills home of Arthur Hiller, the director of *Love Story*, while, as we sat beside her, she appealed (unsuccessfully) for a job. She also expected us to take her to famous (and expensive) restaurants in Beverly Hills and charge it to my *Times* expense account. Abe wouldn't mind, she said, and I don't think he did if he knew about it.

If she wasn't impressed by a restaurant (or the wine I ordered), as was frequently the case, she let us know it with sarcastic indignation, sometimes insultingly, as if she deserved to be treated much better. When we all drove someplace, she insisted that she, not Sandy, sit beside me in the front passenger seat. But after awhile Sandy quickly jumped into the front seat ahead of Katherine, angering her.

She made clear she thought she deserved to be treated *as the wife* of the Executive Editor, not his girlfriend.

And I guess we tried to do so, afraid to alienate Abe.

A couple of days after the dinner party Judi Davidson said she was going to mail me the thank-you note she'd received from Carol Matthau. "What till you see it," she said.

To put it mildly the four page handwritten note was, mysteriously, a gushing rave --how do I say it?--about me and how much she'd enjoyed our conversation.

"He's one of the most interesting men I've met in years," she wrote. *"Do you think they'd come to dinner if I invited them?"*

It was crazy. True, I'd asked Carol a lot of questions and I was a good listener; fellow reporters claimed I had a "Colombo" interviewing style. But I have no idea what could have made me *interesting*, then or now.

This was a woman who, I soon learned, had been a friend of *really* interesting men--Charlie Chaplin, Truman Capote, Neil Simon,

James Agee and virtually every Hollywood leading man of the past thirty years.

I didn't know it when we met but Carol Grace Saroyan Matthau was nearly as well- known as her husband. Capote, a childhood friend, said he had based his character "Holly Golightly," on Carol in his novella, *Breakfast at Tiffany's*. She knew Greta Garbo, had been married not once but twice to author-playwright William Saroyan, and was one of the reigning super-hostesses of Hollywood.

And what an arc her life had taken: Born in 1924 on New York's Lower East Side to an unmarried moneyless 16 year old Jewish girl named Rosheen, she lived in foster homes until she was eight, when Rosheen married multimillionaire Charles Marcus, co-founder of the Bendix Corporation. Literally overnight Carol moved from a foster home into an 18 room Park Avenue apartment, enrolled at Manhattan's uppity Dalton School and entered a world of debutantes, wealth, privilege and glamour.

As a teenager, her best friends were fellow debs Gloria Vanderbilt, the heiress and future fashion queen, and Oona O'Neill, daughter of playwright Eugene O'Neill; as teenagers, they made a vow to each marry a rich and famous man: Oona O' Neill would marry Chaplin; Gloria Vanderbilt married conductor Leopold Stokowski (along with three other husbands later); and Carol married Saroyan.

After two children and lots of marital strife, she divorced Saroyan, married him again, then divorced him again, she told me, because of his compulsive gambling, drinking and emotional and physical abuse of her and her kids. In 1959, seven years after her second divorce, while beginning to have a little success as an actress on Broadway, she married Matthau.

When I met Carol she was in her late fifties and still youthful looking, an attractive blonde who sometimes wore so much skin whitening make-up that she reminded me of a player in a Japanese kabuki drama.

She called a couple of weeks after the Davidsons' party. Like all her calls, it began with a high pitched, long purring of my first name. I never had to ask who was calling.

She invited us to a dinner party at the Matthaus' home in Pacific Palisades to introduce us to some of her friends. We'd be the guests of honor, welcoming us to Southern California. I accepted and said Sandy would probably want to know what to wear.

" She can come naked with her hair on fire as far as I care, I just want the two of you there, to show you off."

Carol met us at the door and led us to the family room where a bartender poured tall flutes of Dom Perignon champagne, then said she wanted to show us something in her garage:

Opening the door she pointed to the license plate on her gleaming blue Rolls Royce : MI6 -- the name of Britain's secret intelligence agency.

"These are my friends I told you about," she said as she led us around the room, introducing us to many of the other guests as proudly as if she was unveiling a gift. She paused when we reached two women talking together at the far side of the room.

One, looking regal in a billowing green silk dress, was Gloria Vanderbilt, the other, dark haired and pretty, was Oona O'Neill, Charlie Chaplin's widow.

They extended their hands and we made small talk. Afterward Sandy and I agreed they must have been thinking: *How did these people get into the party?*

If they didn't roll their eyes, they must have wanted to.

Carol continued around the room, introducing us to Gregory Peck, Neil Simon, Jack Lemmon, directors Sidney Pollack and Billy Wilder, agent Irving Lazar, Carol Channing, Steve Martin, Bernadette Peters and a room full of other celebrities, their spouses and Significant Others.

Left on our own, we drank our champagne and roamed the room observing the other guests. Most, famous or not, glanced at us briefly avoiding eye contact, and when they didn't recognize us, looked away quickly and scanned the space beyond us, searching for more famous faces.

At dinner Walter, sitting at one end of the table where Sandy and I were seated, joked about being a better looking leading man than Warren Beatty while comedienne/director Elaine May lifted up a spoonful of caviar from a hallowed baked potato shell (the dinner appetizer) and while she talked the caviar tumbled off her spoon, leaving a huge black stain covering the front of her blouse; nobody mentioned it and she kept telling funny stories.

Sandy and I were out of our element and well aware of it, insecure outliers feeling uncomfortable and anxious to go home. Still, we were among the last to leave. As we were getting ready to go, Walter suggested he and I shoot a game of Eight Ball on the family room pool table. We played and he won more than once.

27

The evening was the first of many at the Matthaus' homes in Pacific Palisades and Malibu, where we were usually token outsiders at gatherings of actors and other movie people, usually eating bowls of chili catered by Chasen's, then a popular Hollywood hangout, along with fancier items.

Carol usually introduced me as an "investigative reporter" for *The Times*, a misnomer I disliked. After Woodward and Bernstein helped bring down Nixon, many journalists became pumped up with self importance as if they were members of a new class of nobility and called themselves investigative reporters.

"Investigative reporter" is redundant: Any reporter, whether covering a farm town like Gilroy or the Federal bureaucracy in Washington, routinely pursues leads that suggest incompetence, corruption or malfeasance. That's their job. As my high school journalism teacher taught us, journalism was searching for truth; it goes with the territory, a fundamental part of the job, not a separate mission nor justification for a special title.

Dinner conversation at the Matthaus usually featured talk about Hollywood—movies, contracts, disputes with studios or agents-- but occasionally the parties produced a story for *The Times*. Jack Lemmon, a close friend of the Matthaus who sat next to me at one dinner at their Malibu beachfront home, told me a close relative had been diagnosed with a newly recognized symptom of Alzheimer's, resulting in a story for the Science Desk.

A still-closeted actor told me a surprising number of his gay friends were being affected by a mysterious illness, resulting in one of the paper's earliest reports about AIDS. Another evening the Significant Other of a Hollywood star said he was sleepy because he'd been awake most of the previous night communicating with strangers on his computer.

The result was a 1983 story headlined "COMPUTER AS LETTERBOX, SINGLES BAR AND SEMINAR," one of the earliest reports of the coming Internet revolution.

"For thousands of Americans, the personal computer is becoming the ham radio of the 1980's," the story stated, "a forum for dialogues on politics, religion and other matters, matchmaking and courtship. Protected by the anonymity of a computer screen and the length of a cross country telephone line, strangers debate and harangue; shy people lose their shyness; and many people invent fantasy lives about themselves, fabricating identities and accomplishments in the hope of impressing electronic pen pals they never meet."

These dinners also sent me on a few wild goose chases. One of Carol's closest friends, Marge Everett, was among the principal owners of the Hollywood Park racetrack near where I'd grown up and where Walter did a lot of gambling. She claimed that some state regulators of the racing industry were corrupt. After devoting several days to looking into her claims, I found a little smoke but no fire or none I could write about without risking a libel suit.

While working on this story, I drove past the trailer camps near Hollywood Park where I'd spent part of my life. All the trailers were gone. One was now the site of a two story apartment building, the other, behind an iron fence, was vacant except for fifteen concrete slabs in two rows where our trailer and others had once stood, and one larger slab, site of the building that housed our showers and toilets; collectively, they were the archeological ruins of my childhood, and I wondered how much I had left of myself there.

(I wasted more time and my credibility when I wrote a couple of Business section articles about an inventor named Sam Leslie Leach who claimed to have developed a kind of perpetual motion machine— a process to separate the oxygen and hydrogen in water and produce energy despite laws of physics that said it was impossible. Leach was in his late sixties with a full gray beard and an intelligence I found impressive, not to mention a shelf full of patents for previous inventions. He lived in a million dollar ocean front estate in Pebble Beach and drove a pair of expensive Rolls Royce's (given to him, along with another house, by an investor, a Beverly Hills rental car tycoon), not to mention the Dodge he'd modified with his "SLX process" that he said ran on hydrogen generated from his water by his invention. For years I believed and rooted for him, but finally came to the conclusion that he was a very articulate con man and my articles probably helped him lure unsuspecting investors into his scheme It was Lindsey's Folly, my most embarrassing experience as a journalist.)

For most of the next decade, Carol Matthau called often, usually weekly, to gossip, inevitably returning to her passionate obsession with Admiral Wilhelm Franz Canaris, commander of the Abwehr, the World war II German military intelligence service, about whom she was determined to write a book proving *"there was at least one good German."*

Like most people, she found it impossible to understand how Germans--not just the murderous SS but ordinary Germans--not only accepted but participated in Hitler's savage campaign to exterminate Jews. She said she'd had an interest in espionage for as long as she could remember, probably because of what she suspected about her stepfather's mysterious wartime life. She'd read a lot about the war and was convinced Canaris was a double agent working for Britain's MI6 as well as the Abwehr; her suspicion was largely based on a reported meeting in Spain in 1941 or 1942 between Canaris and Sir Stuart Menzies, the head of MI6. She was sure her research would find the *"one good German."*

For reasons I can't explain, she confided candidly and at length about her life and problems, including often intimate aspects of her experiences, using me as a kind of unpaid counselor . She just wanted to talk (so much so I often couldn't shut her up or get off the phone), sometimes about intimate matters I had no right to know about and didn't want to know, ranging from her sex life with Walter (basically very good) and Saroyan (tempestuous, domineering, physically abusive) to Walter's debilitating passion for gambling and their frequent arguments over this or that; she talked about the recurrent financial troubles of her two children by Saroyan and their demands to share Walter's wealth, but also about the goodness of Charlie, her son with Walter. And of course there was always gossip about Hollywood stars ranging from Johnny Carson to Marlon Brando.

I heard one sentence from Carol at least half a dozen times over the years:

"Walter's spent all our money, he's gambled it away; we're broke. "

When Arthur Gelb, then the *Times'* Managing Editor, told me he was coming to L.A. with his wife, Barbara, I invited Carol and Walter to have dinner with them at a swanky restaurant called L'Orangerie. The Gelbs had written the definitive biography of Eugene O'Neill, so they had lots of questions about Carol's friend Oona.

The dinner was a success, and the Gelbs were clearly pleased, but we were all puzzled by Walter's sudden, abrupt disappearance several times during the meal.

Finally, he explained his absences: he'd bet $17,000 on the Los Angeles Lakers that night, and he'd been checking the score of the game.

"How long have you been gambling?," Arthur asked.

"Every day since I was eleven," Walter said.

After moving to a separate bedroom (in part, I think, because of Walter's snoring), Carol began calling me from a telephone she'd had installed secretly under her bed to hide it from Walter. She said she used it daily, often late at night, to chat with Oona, Gloria and other friends and almost nightly to Brando, with whom decades before she'd had a fiery one night stand. Walter knew about the affair and as a result, she said "Walter *loathes* Marlon."

As she opened up about her life, she said her abandonment as a child to a foster home left permanent marks on her emotionally but she was fortunate to have been rescued by her stepfather while Gloria--the target of an infamous child custody battle--and Oona, who'd been cruelly disowned by her alcoholic playwright-father because she married Chaplin against his will, had had it much worse.

The decision by Orion Pictures to film *The Falcon and the Snowman* brought another visit from Katherine Balfour. She was convinced she was the perfect actress to play the mother of either Christopher Boyce or Daulton Lee in the movie and urged me to arrange an audition. Abe asked me to do what I could. I said I'd try, thinking probably the last thing a casting director wanted was an author's recommendation on who should have a role in the film. Still. I recommended Katherine to John Schlesinger, the director, citing her good reviews in *Summer and Smoke* and Elia Kazan's movie, *America, America*.

Whether she ever auditioned for the movie, I don't remember, but she didn't get either part and once again Sandy and I had to deal with her disappointment, whining and depression.

The day her agent broke the news that she wouldn't get either part we took her to dinner at one of the Beverly Hills restaurants she liked most.

I'll always remember her sadness that night.

"I had so much *potential*," she cried, tears falling on her cheeks, then repeated herself: *"I had so much potential!"*

Sandy and I, meanwhile, had begun noticing fissures in her relationship with Abe.

Katherine never stopped complaining to us about how she'd put her career on hold because Abe had promised to divorce Ann and marry her but inevitably found an excuse to avoid a divorce court, usually blaming it on Ann's recurring health problems.

One night in New York Abe and Katherine (who by then were less secretive about their affair) took us to Elaine's, a then popular hangout of media personalities.

Later,, when we were back at our hotel, Sandy and I agreed the bickering between Abe and Katherine was becoming so intense it had been impossible to enjoy our meal.

As the evening passed he became increasingly annoyed with Katherine, starting when she tried to choose his meal from the menu because she claimed he'd been eating too much butter and cream. Little things rankled him. When she absent- mindedly toyed with her eyeglasses on the table in front of her he said twice:

"Why do you do that all the time?"

It seemed to us we were witnessing a long love affair beginning to unravel.

In the weeks that followed, Katherine was on the phone a lot, seeking our sympathy and complaining how Abe was treating her badly, asking us to agree with her and going into their sex life far more deeply than we wanted to hear. It was an uncomfortable time in my life.

28

More than a year and a half after Christopher Boyce disappeared over the razor-wire topped fences at the Lompoc penitentiary, one of the Deputy U.S. Marshals searching for him called me at the *Times* Bureau and said he wanted to show me some pictures .

I invited him to lunch at a nearby Japanese restaurant where he laid out several photos taken by security cameras at different banks on the table in front of us.

They showed a man sticking a gun in the face of bank tellers. Although in each grainy image he wore a different hat or a wig, I recognized the same man in every picture; it was *Christopher Boyce.*

I couldn't believe it.

Chris hated guns and violence, or so I thought. He was a pacifist, or so I thought. It couldn't be him.

The Deputy Marshal said Chris was a suspect in at least 16 bank robberies in Idaho and Washington state.

Flabbergasted?

It was too mild a word to explain how I felt.

Chris couldn't be Jesse James.

He hadn't fired the gun during the robberies. But what would have happened if a guard or a bank customer tried to wrest it from him?

The Chris I knew--or thought I knew-- was an idealist who'd fallen almost accidentally into one of the most damaging incidents of espionage in the country since World War II; a victim, I thought, of a desire to expose government duplicity following the debacle of the Vietnam War, as well as Daulton Lee's persuasion and intimidation.

I'd occasionally had doubts but ignored them. One of Chris' inmate friends   told me after his escape that he and Chris had hatched a plan (obviously never carried out) to murder Daulton Lee because for some reason Chris thought it would speed up his parole if Lee was dead. Nor did I pay much attention to the former friend of Chris from Palos Verdes who claimed I'd been too kind to him and too harsh on Lee in the book, and did I know that one of Chris' favorite ways of providing raw meat for his falcons was to hurl kittens at a garage door to smash them to death?

Whatever the truth of these stories, the bank security cameras revealed a Christopher Boyce I had badly misjudged.

29

Several months later-- after almost 21 month as a fugitive in Idaho and Washington--Chris was arrested at a drive in restaurant in Port Angeles, Washington by deputy marshals. He'd been betrayed by two former confederates from his career as a bank robber.

The night Chris was arrested I flew to Seattle and visited him in his cell. As his lawyers and deputy marshals watched, we hugged, then he autographed copies of *Falcon* for his jailers. I spent about an hour with him and mentioned the story I'd heard about his supposed partnership with another inmate to kill Daulton. He met my eyes coldly, then looked away without responding.

He was tried and convicted of 16 counts of armed robbery and escaping from prison and sentenced to 28 years in addition to the unfinished portion of his original sentence of 40 years.

When Simon & Schuster asked me to write a sequel to *Falcon* about Boyce's escape and the ensuing manhunt, I agreed, and Chris and I briefly resumed our former dance: he called me collect and we discussed his life on the run. After members of a right wing prison gang, the Aryan Brotherhood, beat him savagely at the Leavenworth, Kansas federal penitentiary, he called, barely able to speak, and asked me to tell his parents and lawyers about the beating. Because of the attack, the lawyers arranged for a transfer to a penitentiary in Marion, Illinois (later he was moved to high security prisons in Minnesota and eventually to the nation's most secure Federal prison in Florence, Colorado) with Chris all the while urging me to abandon the second book.

I suspect that after the beating he longed for a low profile in the brutal prison culture, but I told him it was too late: I'd already signed a contract to write a second book. He wasn't happy. From then on he refused to tell me anything more about his escapades and continued asking me to give up the book, but I pushed ahead, beginning the end of our collaboration and friendship.

Without his cooperation, I turned to the marshals who had hunted for him around the world as the basis for the new book, casting them as the protagonists of the story while portraying Chris as I now saw him-- a reckless, risk taking, gun-wielding serial bank robber who terrified bank tellers and customers.

After the sequel, *The Flight of the Falcon,* was published, Chris wrote me a terse good-by letter, accusing me of betraying our friendship and telling me he had told prison authorities to return my letters unopened.

As this was happening a debate was beginning to take shape about the ethics of journalists, especially writers of "non fiction novels."

The debate was touched off by Janet Malcolm, a writer for the *New Yorker,* who accused journalists of disingenuously and often deceitfully seducing subjects into trusting and cooperating with them.

"Every journalist who is not too stupid or too full of himself to notice what is going on knows that what he does is morally indefensible," the book began. "

The journalist, she argued, "is a kind of confidence man, preying on people's vanity, ignorance or loneliness, gaining their trust and betraying them without remorse....the consenting subject of a piece of nonfiction learns--when the article or book appears--his hard lesson. Journalists justify their treachery in various ways according to their temperaments. The more pompous talk about freedom of speech and 'the public's right to know.' The least talented talk about Art; the seemliest murmur about earning a living."

I'd made (at least) two mistakes in writing the *Falcon and the Snowman*. Because of his charm and likeability, I misjudged Chris' character—I never expected him to be a bank robber--and I became too close to him, a friend instead of objective journalist.

But was I guilty of the kind of unsavory manipulation Janet Malcolm described?

Anne Lee, Daulton's mother, who had always insisted she knew nothing about her son's prosperous drug business and had doubts about his guilt in the alleged espionage, came to my home for a drink after *The Falcon and the Snowman* was published. She enjoyed the book, she said, but added, "I tried to help you and you stabbed me in the back." She'd expected me to write a book that would exonerate her son and in fact I'd written about his drug business and dealings with Soviet KGB agents.

For a long while I had also been close to Chris' mother, Noreen Boyce, speaking to her often and passing messages between her and her son. I never thought of myself as "using" her. But with publication of *The Flight of the Falcon* after she'd helped my research with *The Falcon and the Snowman* perhaps she could argue that I'd betrayed her trust.

Still, aren't journalists ethically obligated to report the truth wherever it leads them?

In any case, Chris asked her after the second book was published to end her friendship with me, and she did.

Was I a con man? Without a doubt I tried to butter up the two protagonists of the story, their parents and lawyers, offering them friendship in exchange for information. I tried to induce them to trust and talk to me. I tried to make them like me. I just thought I was doing my job.

Was I guilty of the kind of "treachery" cited by Malcolm?

Maybe.

Maybe not.

Chris Boyce, after being paroled in 2002, married and moved to Central Oregon, where he resumed his passion for falconry.

Daulton Lee, with a record of good behavior in prison, had been paroled several years earlier and hired by Sean Penn, the actor who portrayed him in *The Falcon and the Snowman* movie, as a personal assistant.

30

At a conference of *Times* correspondents I hosted in San Francisco Abe Rosenthal asked to be seated next to Sandy at dinner. They spent most of the meal conversing head to head as if no one else was in the room and at one point he took her face in his two hands and kissed her on the lips.

As the dinner broke up, Abe came to me glowing, put his arm on my shoulder and said:

"Be nice to Sandy. She's very special."

On the sidewalk outdoors , I asked her:

"What was that all about?"

"I think I gave him permission to leave Katherine."

From our college days (even in high school, I'm told) Sandy had often served as a kind of counselor to her friends. She was a good listener and analytical when evaluating people's feelings and motives, and they often followed her advice.

Later that night she described her conversation with Abe:

"He said he wasn't happy. Katherine was still trying to get work and leaning too much on him, blaming him for her problems, expecting him to be responsible for restarting her career. She was very needy. He hated being responsible for her.

"I told him maybe you need a more independent woman who has her own life and feels good about herself and doesn't depend on you for her happiness."

She told Abe he was entitled to have his own happiness and Katherine--an unhappy, clinging woman may not be the answer for him, and "you shouldn't feel guilty about it."

Within a few weeks, Abe ended the affair that had lasted for close to fifteen years and sent Sandy a note thanking her for what she'd said, then a second one.

He promoted me to management status at the paper, adding perks, retirement benefits and pay raises that he said made me the highest paid correspondent at the *Times*. Whether Sandy's counseling was a factor, I'll never know, although in one letter mentioning he'd put through an additional raise for me, he wrote:

"I really can't tell you how much that conversation with Sandy meant to me. I rely upon you and your warm, loving and sensitive wife to understand.

"Fondly,

Abe."

About the time Abe was breaking up with Katherine she learned Sandy and I were in New York and called the Wyndham Hotel where we were staying and asked Sandy to lunch.

"You'll pay for it, won't you?," she said. "Bob can put it on his expense account."

Sandy said she didn't think I could. "Why don't we just have coffee?, she said.

"I don't do coffee" Katherine said.

That was the last time either of us spoke to her.

A year later, Abe, then nearly 65 and approaching the *Times'* mandatory retirement age for executives, divorced Ann and tried to persuade Punch Sulzberger to waive the policy and let him remain Executive Editor a few more years.

Aware of the morale problems Abe had induced on the staff, the publisher turned him down but offered him a twice a week column on the opinion page.

Less than a year after divorcing Ann, Abe married the kind of woman Sandy had described--Shirley Lord, a British-born novelist and fashion journalist with the self- assuredness, independence and history of achievement Sandy's said he needed but didn't find in Katherine.

Shirley helped turn him into a new man, choosing him a new wardrobe, new glasses and a new look, and they became fixtures in New York society, often photographed with friends like Barbara Walters and Beverly Sills.

Unlike his glamorous new social life, Abe's column, *"On My Mind*," was not a big success.

Much of what he wrote were the self-centered, egotistical rantings of a know-it- all, a self-appointed oracle who did little new reporting and repeated almost identical themes week after week.

After almost 13 years, Sulzberger ordered his column killed. Abe said he was called into the publisher's office and told: "It's time."

"What that means, I don't know," he told an interviewer for the *Washington Post*.

"I didn't expect it at all," he added, reminding me again of the editor I met on one of my first days in New York who said:

"I have several rules about The New York Times. One of them is that sooner or later it will break your heart."

Abe then risked more ridicule by offering his column to the *Times'* low brow rival, the *New York Daily News,* which published it for four years before he finally gave it up.

Katherine Balfour, bitter and almost destitute after failing to revive her acting career and trying to make a living as a magazine writer and a radio talk show host, died in 1990, at 69 of amyotrophic lateral sclerosis, Lou Gehrig's Disease.

When I read about her death in the *Times*, I thought of her sad words repeated so often: *"I had so much potential,"*

Abe Rosenthal suffered a stroke in 2006 and died two weeks later at the age of 84.

When he died I hadn't seen him in more than two years. The last time was when I'd invited Abe and Arthur Gelb, who had also retired, to a reunion of *Times* National Correspondents in New York. During a brief talk to the group, I praised the two of them for making the sweeping changes in the paper that had kept it in business and saved the jobs of all the correspondents in the room.

Afterward, Shirley Lord and Abe, greyer and more jowly than I remembered, offered Sandy and me a ride from the restaurant to the Wyndham.

As we all got out of their limousine to say our goodbyes outside the hotel, Shirley touched me warmly and said: "Thanks so much for what you said, Bob. He needs it, and I appreciate it."

31

From the beginning our dream was to live in San Francisco overlooking the Golden Gate Bridge. In 1985 we arrived there when I was appointed San Francisco-based Chief West Coast Correspondent of *The Times,* given a brief to write about anything I wanted around the country and a deep pocketed expense account . (This was, after all, long before the Internet sent the newspaper industry into a tailspin of cost cutting and layoffs.)

About the time we moved north to San Francisco from L.A. something curious began happening: people I had known long ago or worked with years before started calling me to let me know they'd been visited by private investigators who wanted to know everything about me.

Calls came in from all over the country. Young women who'd worked as my assistants in the L.A. Bureau said they had been asked whether I'd harassed them sexually; investigators visited Boyce and Lee in prison and the leaders of the U.S. Marshals Service in Washington asking if there were errors in the *Falcon* books and to glean any dirt they could use against me. One investigator sent two pages of questions to Boyce before visiting him in prison, including the final one: "Are there any friends/associates/family you know that could have information about Lindsey, and who will talk to me about him?"

Bill Kamrath, my high school journalism teacher, wrote to tell me had been interviewed "by an investigator, a handsome, pleasant man in his 30's who never did get through to me exactly what his function is, though he is involved somehow in biographical work about authors. He wanted to know Bob Lindsey as I know and knew him, sending me down a frantic trip to memory lane."

How in the world did they discover I'd been taught by this obscure, long -retired high school teacher more than thirty years before?

Somehow the "investigators" even managed to track down my mother in law who lived in a little-known retirement community in Northern California.

It was creepy, maybe even scary. I was getting calls from friends all over the country with the same report; it must have been costing *someone* thousands and thousands of dollars. What was going on?

I began piecing together what was happening: With a little research I discovered two of the "investigators" were former Los Angeles and Riverside County police detectives who worked for the "church" of Scientology. I realized I had been targeted for what Scientologists called the "Fair Game Doctrine."

In the 1950's, L. Ron Hubbard, a penny-a-word pulp magazine science fiction writer, had established a network of mental health clinics that he would later rename the "Church of Scientology" after mentioning during a lecture:

"If a man really wants to make a million dollars, the best way would be to start his own religion."

I'd spent a good part of the 1980s writing about the organization because of a seemingly unlimited river of disaffected insiders coming forth claiming that the "church" was actually a hugely profitable, franchised business that amassed millions under the disguise of a First Amendment- protected religion, intimidating anyone who criticized it. I'd written front page stories about huge amounts of money being moved to foreign bank accounts, touching off an I.R.S. investigation. I'd taken one self described defector out to lunch at the paper's expense before realizing he was a member of the "church" attempting to learn the sources for several of these stories.

Hubbard had declared that anyone who was a threat to the "church" was "fair game" to be attacked in retaliation by the organization, using whatever means available, including lawsuits and private investigators to investigate critics. "Hire them and damn the cost when you need to," he was quoted as telling his aides:

"Always find or manufacture enough threat against them to cause them to sue for peace. Don't ever defend. Always attack."

It dawned on me that it had been relatively easy for me to learn the identity of the detectives who were going around the country asking about me. Perhaps Scientology *wanted* me to know what it was doing, so I'd lay off what I was doing.

The Scientologists pulled off their hounds only after I decided to retire:

I hadn't realized it when we moved to a fourteenth floor apartment overlooking the Golden Gate and Alcatraz in 1985, achieving our goal, but I was starting to burn out as a reporter.

I never aspired to be an editor—editors didn't have nearly as much fun as reporters—but I was under growing pressure to take an editing job in New York. When Sandy and I were in Mexico City to watch the filming of *The Falcon and the Snowman*, Arthur Gelb called me off the movie set to offer me the job of *Times* Sports Editor. I suspect he thought that since I'd covered the 1984 Olympics in Los Angeles and written articles about Oakland Raiders Managing Partner Al Davis and Olympic ice skaters for the Sunday magazine that I was a wannabe sports editor. I was never a sports fanatic and told him I wanted to remain a reporter. Two days after we returned from Mexico he called and said he wanted to promote me to deputy editor of the Sunday Magazine, an interim step before assuming the editorship. It was a job that offered great perks: among others, two tickets for every new show opening on Broadway, but again I declined. About the same time, Foreign Editor Warren Hoge offered me perhaps the paper's choicest foreign assignment, Bureau Chief in London.

I kept working at the job in San Francisco—also prized in newspaper journalism--for three years. But I was continuing to lose my competitiveness and my compulsion to get my byline on the front page every day. The internal locomotive that had propelled me since Gilroy was running out of steam.

Editors' story suggestions started to bore me. I went to news conferences and sat next to ambitious reporters the age of my children, adding to my midlife malaise. Although I was still more enterprising than many correspondents, the thrill was gone, and if I kept it up, I knew I'd be yanked back to New York and lose control of my destiny.

I still remembered the burned-out, once respected correspondents assigned to the back of the City Room in New York I met during my first days at the paper waiting to die or retire while writing as few insignificant stories as they could get away with.

And I still remembered the promise I'd made to myself never to be an "old reporter," nor did I forget the editor's dictum: *"Sooner or later the New York Times will break your heart."*

Candidly, I wanted to quit before consistently making a fool of myself.

I was bothered by another problem: I'd sprouted a big head: After my brief moments of fame--"a minor celebrity" as *People* Magazine put it -- I'd started believing my own publicity. When a couple of people I interviewed said they were "honored" to meet me because of the books I'd written it was flattering but discomforting. When I interviewed Stansfield Turner , a former C.I.A. director, about an epidemic of espionage cases, he immediately quoted *me* as a source of expertise about why Americans committed espionage. I had to remind him who he was talking to.

And during interviews for articles I was writing for the *Times'* Sunday Magazine about movie director Francis Ford Coppola and TV producer Stephen Bochco, I unconsciously shifted from asking questions about them to mentioning my own work. I'd become someone I disliked and mocked: a journalist who likes fame.

After the two '"Falcon" books, I wrote *"A Gathering of Saints,* about two murders in Salt Lake City and the nearly successful efforts by a master forger to upend the Mormon church. I was helped enormously by a Salt Lake detective, Michael George, a Catholic who helped me navigate the distinctive, often peculiar culture of Mormon Utah.

The book was generally well received and Alice Mayhew, my editor at Simon & Schuster, pressed me to write another.

When I told other *Times* correspondents that I was thinking about retiring from the paper at the age of 53 because I wasn't as sharp as I once was, they said I was nuts. (I suspect some of those around my age felt they were losing their drive too, but didn't want to acknowledge it. A reporter-friend on *The Washington Post* told me: "The worst thing you can tell your editor is that you're 'burning out;'

you can say you're an alcoholic or a drug user or an adulterer and you'll keep your job. Once you say you're 'burned out' you're through.")

There was an added reason I decided to leave at 53. Abe Rosenthal had retired, a new executive editor, Max Frankel, and other new editors were in place, and I preferred the old regime. Abe had been my "rabbi," as they say in New York. He'd looked out for me. I didn't know what to expect from the new gang, even though I'd been offered a place in the new leadership. When I told Frankel I didn't want to move to New York to become National Editor, Dave Jones' successor after he'd received a promotion, I knew sooner or later Frankel would deduce I'd lost my steam. When that happened, I knew I'd lose control over our lives and where we lived.

Frankel and Gelb refused to accept my resignation and informed the *Times'* Human Resources Department I would be taking a Leave of Absence, enabling me to return to the reporting staff at my current salary, management status and benefit package if I changed my mind.

Sandy and I moved to a home we'd bought for our retirement in Carmel on the Monterey Peninsula not far from where we met and later became engaged many years before, and we began a new phase of our lives.

The first book I decided to write as a full time author had its roots in a pair of visits by one of Sandy's high school friends. On the first visit he described how his niece, Monika Zumsteg, had fallen in love with a young British tourist, married him and when they moved to England, she discovered his family was worth billions, with a fortune second in size only to that of the British royal family, and how they'd settled into a home in a quaint English village called West Wickham.

On his second visit to Carmel a year later he told us the Cinderella story had turned into a Gothic horror tale referred to by the British press as "The Headless Corpse Case."

I liked reading Agatha Christie- style murder mysteries set in charming English villages and decided the life and death of Monika Zumsteg would be my next project, but before long Carol Matthau called and said:

"Baaaaaoob?

"I have a friend who would like to talk to you. Do you mind if I give him your number?"

"No."

A few minutes later my phone rang and I heard a voice I'd listened to many times while enveloped in the shadows of a movie theater.

"This is Marlon Brando."

"Hi," I said.

Brando wanted to make me an offer I wouldn't want to refuse.

PART TWO

32

Marlon said he was calling to ask me to write a book but couldn't discuss the particulars yet because he suspected his phone was bugged. If I visited him in Beverly Hills he'd tell me the details.

For a (former) reporter, his call was like an invitation to the headwaters of the Nile to meet the ghost of Dr. Livingston. Brando was probably the most secretive and reclusive Hollywood star since Mary Pickford, living alone in a hilltop aerie on Mulholland Drive, turning away producers who sent him scripts, refusing to return telephone messages, ignoring his mail and biographers' and journalists' appeals for interviews.

For decades he had been called "the greatest actor in the world" largely because of his stage and film work as a young man, starting with his explosive performance in *A Streetcar Named Desire* and reaching its peak about the time he starred in *The Wild One* and *On the Waterfront*. After a few well regarded films and a longer string of clunkers his star peaked again with his1972 Oscar- winning performance in *The Godfather*, followed by *Last Tango in Paris*.

If he wanted me to help write a book, I imagined it could be lucrative: He had not made a movie in seven or eight years; he had simply vanished, adding to his mystique and legend that, I thought, might attract a large publisher's advance.

When I told him I'd fly to L.A. in several days, he gave me his address-- 12900 Mulholland Drive-- and said the front gate would be locked and I was to push a button on a post next to the road, identify myself and the gate would open; then I was to drive down a hill "and magic will happen."

When I got there I pushed a button and heard an angry, cranky voice.

"Who is it?"

I gave my name and said Marlon was expecting me.

"You pushed the wrong button!"

It was Marlon's neighbor, Jack Nicholson, who lived on the same hill. I'd awakened him, making him an unhappy neighbor.

I pushed a different button and the woman who answered--I later learned it was Marlon's housekeeper, Christina Ruiz-- opened the gate by remote control.

The winding, downhill road ahead of me was surrounded both sides by forests of bamboo and trees. After a few hundred yards I still hadn't seen any structures. Then the forest on my left began to move. A second gate hidden by tall greenery planted in its base swung open slowly, revealing a cluster of buildings at the top of a hill and two big dogs bounding toward me. A sign near the top of the hill warned visitors to remain in their vehicles or risk attack by the dogs, a boxer and a mastiff, until an escort arrived.

Marlon's home and several smaller buildings were perched atop one of the famous Beverly Hills. To the east the vast panorama of the San Fernando Valley stretched to infinity; to the west, rolling hills descended into the sprawl of the Los Angeles Basin. I imagined the view would be stunning at night when a blanket of twinkling lights came alive in every direction.

Besides a single story home that suggested an Asian designer, there was a guest house, a separate workshop and several other outbuildings including a cottage I later learned was designated for Brando's office staff.

I followed instructions and sat in my car until a gardener holding a rake came over and said the dogs wouldn't hurt me, and as if to prove he was right, the two big animals came over and licked my hands.

33

It was late morning and Marlon was asleep. Christina said she'd wake him, and a half hour later he entered the living room sleepy eyed and wearing the identical outfit he would wear during dozens of future visits: a loose fitting blue and white cotton kimono that barely covered his bulging girth, an obi tied loosely around his huge waist, a white tee shirt, white jockey shorts and fuzzy-wuzzy sheepskin slippers .

When he sat down he said we'd discuss the book project in a few minutes.

Even though I was no longer a *Times* correspondent, I'd dressed in the uniform of a *Times* reporter: blue blazer, button down shirt, necktie, slacks and polished dark shoes.

"Where'd you get those Buster Brown shoes?"

That's how he introduced himself.

"What do you mean?"

"*Laces*. You have lace up shoes."

Carol Matthau, he said, had given me the strongest of recommendations, but since I'd written a book involving the C.I.A., he wondered if I worked for the agency. He pointed to a hilltop half a mile away that bristled with antenna masts; government agents, he said, could easily eavesdrop on our conversation by penetrating electronically the glass walls of the Japanese style home that he said had once been owned by Howard Hughes.

"Guess so," I said.

I discovered Marlon was the most curious person I'd ever met. As I sat in one plush sofa and he in a matching one a few feet away, a coffee table between us, he began peppering me with questions --about my friendship with Carol, my family, my childhood, the books I'd written, the books I'd read, my religious views, what I thought about the Israeli-Palestinian conflict, whether I thought chimpanzees would ever be taught to communicate directly with humans.

When I answered his questions I could tell he was really *listening,* usually following up with more questions, paying me the kind of attention that made me feel he was really interested in my answers.

We'd been at it for about an hour when he asked:

" How'd you get along with your father?," a topic I later learned was close to his heart.

I answered candidly:
"He was an alcoholic who molested me sexually when I was a kid."

Perhaps after his intense grilling I wanted to shock him. Otherwise I don't know why I was so candid.

Marlon may have been the greatest actor of his generation but sometimes he was unable to conceal his emotions as much as he thought he did. Usually when he was surprised by something but didn't want to show it his eyes froze for the briefest moment, there was a split second of silence, then he'd move on as if what he'd just heard was ordinary.

Gingerly, probably with some embarrassment, he probed for details about my father, but I added only a few.

He said he wanted to show me a biofeedback system that measured galvanic skin response--in other words, sweat—that he used during his daily meditation to measure the degree of his relaxation. He hooked me up to the gadget and asked more questions. It worked, he said, like a polygraph machine and could detect lies; after a few more questions he said I'd passed his makeshift polygraph exam.

I said it was his turn and asked him to attach himself to it .

He hadn't made a movie in years. Why? I asked.

"Didn't need the money."

"Are you planning to write an autobiography? It could be very interesting."

(This was me trying to set up what I hoped would be a profitable endeavor.)

"*Never.*

The needle on the instrument didn't react, suggesting he was being truthful.

"I despise people who do that to get attention, going into all the secrets, all because of a prurient interest in celebrities, I'll never do it. It's disgusting."

I asked about his children. He said he had "ten or eleven."

From what I'd read some of these kids, especially his 35 year old son Christian, target of a bitter custody battle between Marlon and one of his ex-wives, Anna Kafshi, had had difficult childhoods.

Christian, Marlon claimed, was the victim of a "crazy" childhood, drank too much and took too many drugs. But he was trying to turn his life around. Marlon had bought him acreage in Washington and he was learning to be a welder, living there while welding metal art pieces.

"Do you think you've been a good father?

"Yes," he said, his eyes closed.

"Their problem is the name of their father. If they fuck up, they get their names in the paper because of who their father is."

The instrument seemed to indicate he didn't feel guilt about his children's difficulties but I heard pain in his voice when he described how his daughter Cheyenne had recently been seriously injured in an automobile accident in Tahiti.

"She got into drugs," he said.

"What kind?"

"You name it."

Cheyenne's mother was the Tahitian beauty Tarita whom Brando met during the filming of *Mutiny on the Bounty* in the 1960s. He said they'd been married in a Tahitian tribal ceremony.

Before the accident Cheyenne told him she wanted to fly to California to visit but he had turned her down. According to police officials in French Polynesia, Cheyenne then drove off in her jeep at more than 90 miles an hour, missed a turn and crashed into a tree.

Until the accident, Marlon said Cheyenne had begun establishing herself as a model but her face was badly disfigured in the crash and even though he'd hired the best plastic surgeons he could find to reconstruct her features she was depressed over what had happened to her.

Still, her problems were deeper than her facial injuries, he added.

She'd been using drugs for so long they "cooked her brain." .

Christina brought in a late lunch of grilled salmon, and for the first time I realized how really fat Marlon was. As we sat across from each other on our respective sofas, he ate from a plate of salmon parked securely on his *huge* stomach as if it were a table. Between bites, I kept waiting for the plate to tumble down his gut and the fish to fall on the floor, but it stayed put as if it was glued there.

I finally asked him to tell me about the book project that brought me to Beverly Hills, and he told me a story:

In the early 1970's, a beautiful Eurasian woman --part Chinese, part Russian-- met the author James Clavell in Hong Kong and she became his mistress. The married Australian-born Clavell was author of the bestselling book, *King Rat,* which he said was based on his personal experiences during World War II as a POW at the Changi, Singapore, prison camp; other best sellers, including *Shogun,* followed.

In 1972 after Clavell's mistress, Caroline Barrett, gave birth to a daughter, Petra, he abandoned both of them with little money and refused to acknowledge he was the child's father.

Caroline and Petra found their way to Los Angeles where she became, for awhile, Marlon's mistress. Their sexual relationship had ended and Caroline now worked for him full time as his personal assistant.

Marlon legally adopted Petra, who was now a teenager, and he had spent almost a decade and a million dollars on lawyers and detectives in a campaign to force Clavell to admit he was Petra's father. But after all those years and all that money Clavell was still refusing to acknowledge paternity.

Brando's long running lawsuit aimed at forcing Clavell to acknowledge fatherhood was being adjudicated at a Los Angeles County court in Santa Monica although it had never been publicized because proceedings in juvenile court were sealed.

Marlon wanted me to write a book exposing Clavell as a fraud and force him to acknowledge he was Petra's biological father and give her his name. He said he had thousands of documents to help me research the story including all the records of the Santa Monica court proceedings, reports of detectives from around the world who'd shadowed Clavell and his family and surveillance reports from several former British SAS commandos (and one former CIA agent) he'd hired to gather information that, at least to Marlon, suggested Clavell had lied about his past and may not ever have been imprisoned at Changi.

Marlon's face reddened as he finished the story and said he had decided to "devote my life" to getting revenge for Petra and give her a proper surname. He was clearly a man possessed by outrage.

Was I interested in writing a book on his legal battle with Clavell?

I said I was.

"A battle between 'titans," huh?, " he said, his eyes drifting toward the nearby mountain topped by antenna masts, seeming to savor the moment.

"Yeah."

By now I had to leave for the airport and a plane home and Marlon had to get ready to go out. Michael Jackson, who employed Marlon's son Miko as a bodyguard, had invited him to a concert at the Universal City Amphitheater. As I was leaving, the forested gate swing open and as I went down the hill a long white limousine sent by Jackson pulled up l towards the house.

Two weeks later, a UPS truck arrived at my home and left almost a ton of paper, at least 50 cartons of photocopied documents. Every deposition and legal complaint and stipulation from the case going back nearly a decade had been copied by Marlon's law firm.

(Given lawyers' reputation for overcharging for photocopying I'm sure the cost was enormous.)

There were   reports from Pinkerton detective agency branches around the world documenting surveillance of Clavell and reports detailing investigators' search for dirt on Clavell that Marlon said he would use to "destroy" him.   (I couldn't help but be reminded of my experience with Scientologists.)

I called Marlon and said I had begun reading the material and was sure a book was there to be written, and we agreed to meet again at his home so I could begin interviewing him for the project.

As I began the interviews, I started to realize what a complicated person he was: he was at once a charmer and a controller intent on rigidly managing everyone and everything around him, including me; lazy, he was repelled by anything approaching work; he could be generous, sending me expensive electronic gadgets, or frugal, seemingly always feuding with lawyers or plumbers over what he thought were excessive fees "because I live on Mulholland Drive."

He could be extravagant and naïve about money, almost childlike. He described how he'd lost millions on investments run by scam artists, often for vague environmental projects or liberal causes, and it didn't seem to bother him because he said he'd always been able to make more money by making another movie.

When it came to women, his morals were those of a feral hog, with a history of "lay 'em and leave 'em" encounters, I'd learn, that had left countless women emotionally devastated and a couple suicidal. Yet he thought of himself as a person of high moral standards demonstrated by his work for blacks, American Indians and untouchables in India.

He was contemptuous of any authority that affected him and anarchistic about society's conventions and rules and said that if he hadn't drifted into acting "I would have been a con man." He was vindictive and nasty to anyone whom he thought betrayed him or he perceived of as his enemy. He was well read, but refused to read anything about himself; his memory was so deep he could recite Shakespeare non-stop for an hour or recall vividly his day to day experiences as a teenager with a father whom he hated.

All at the same time, I'd learn, he could be paranoid and kind and vulnerable.

On one visit I asked my son, Steve, who lived in the San Fernando Valley, to drop me at Marlon's for several hours of interviews. Afterward, I said I was going to call Steve to ask him to pick me up but Marlon offered to drive me to his home. Not far from Marlon's house we encountered a car stalled in the middle of a darkened Mulholland Drive. The car's battery had died and the young couple in the car didn't know what to do. Within seconds Marlon stopped, pulled a jumper cord from the trunk of his Lexus and started their car. The couple drove away gratefully, apparently not realizing they'd been rescued by one of the world's best known actors.

Although I told Marlon I'd write the book he wanted, in my heart I was starting to have doubts. Alice Mayhew, my Simon & Schuster editor, also had doubts. Caroline, meanwhile, hinted she wasn't anxious to see details of her story in print because of the potential effect it would have on Petra, who would soon be applying for college. And I knew if I published information from the sealed juvenile court documents, I might be held in contempt of court or worse. And Alice reminded me I still owed her the book about the life and death of Monika Zumsteg.

I told Marlon I needed to take a month or so off from our project while Sandy and I went to England to research the book about Monika that became *Irresistible Impulse*. (The title referred to the temporary insanity defense offered by Monika's husband, Michael Telling, for his decision to shoot Monika, then cut off her head.)

In a brilliant defense financed by Telling's wealthy family, George Carman, one of London's best known (and most expensive) barristers, figuratively placed Monika in the dock, describing her as a bisexual gold digger who humiliated Michael and instilled in him an irresistible impulse to kill her. Britain's garish tabloid press enthusiastically picked up the theme and seemed to want to convince the nation Monika deserved to die. Her husband was acquitted on a murder charge and escaped with a manslaughter conviction based on Carman's defense of "diminished responsibility."

At home I'd always found it easy to convince lawyers, judges, detectives and others to help me during research for a book. But when I arrived in Exeter, site of Telling's trial, court officials said British law required all but superficial records about the case sealed for 25 years. I tracked down the trial's court reporter-stenographer, who had retired in Scotland, and commissioned her to prepare a transcript of the trial from her notes, which luckily she'd kept. Two retired detectives and officials of the Devon and Cornwall Constabulary offered a little help, while several of Monika's British friends helped fill in some of the details of her life in Britain. Still, wandering around England on unfamiliar turf looking for retired policemen and Monika's former friends while coping with an unfamiliar legal system made me miss *The Times*. And unfortunately once again I bent journalism's unwritten ethical rules by becoming too close to those I was writing about. Before going to England, I spent hours with Monika's parents in California while they tried to understand the pillorying of their daughter in the British press. In England, I discovered Monika *may* (or may not) have had a fleeting affair with a British woman during her marriage to Michael, as his lawyer claimed. But the evidence was mixed: I could never find anyone to confirm she was bisexual; on the contrary, her friends in England and California all called her strictly heterosexual. In the book, I acknowledged but played down the lesbian theme mounted by Carman, not wanting to load more pain on to her parents whom I'd grown to like, but maybe diluting my obligation to search for the facts wherever they led me.

Despite some difficulties, the experience let me fulfill my fantasy about writing an Agatha Christie-style mystery in a charming British village and I came home prepared to undertake the Clavell project. But after Sandy and I returned, Alice Mayhew asked me to help Ronald Reagan write his autobiography.

I called Marlon and told him I'd be delayed again writing the book about his battle with Clavell. He wasn't happy .

34

It was St. Patrick's Day in 1989 when I arrived at the Reagan home in the swanky Bel Air section of Los Angeles and passed through a Secret Service-manned gate with Mort Janklow, the former President's agent.

Shortly after Reagan had left office two months before, Janklow had negotiated a multi- million-dollar contract with Simon & Schuster for Reagan to produce two books-- a volume of his speeches and an autobiography covering his life and presidency.

Janklow said the former president had started writing the memoir on his own, filling about 30 pages of a yellow, legal size tablet with handwritten recollections, but he and Nancy Reagan concluded he needed help.

Over lunch before going to the house, Janklow said I was assured of getting the job if I didn't screw up the upcoming meeting. Later I learned I had already been the subject of--and passed-- an intensive vetting operation to determine whether I was a safe candidate to help Reagan, especially given my roots at the liberal *New York Times*. Janklow, Reagan aides and Nancy Reagan questioned campaign staffers who remembered me from 1980 and agreed I'd been even handed and accurate while covering Reagan.

If I got the job, I knew my reputation among friends at the *Times* would take a hit. I was opting to become a mercenary. To work for Reagan—for any politician-- was to work for the enemy, a form of journalistic prostitution.

But I was looking forward to helping write history.

As a uniformed maid opened the front door I saw to my left a figure wearing a green hat and dancing a jig. It was Reagan celebrating St. Patrick's Day and setting a relaxed, genial mood for our meeting.

The next hour was as close to an out of body experience as I'd experienced since arriving in New York City and waiting to be interviewed by the likes of Scotty Reston and Abe Rosenthal and beginning to realize the unthinkable—a job at *The New York Times* was a possibility.

After eight years, Reagan had left the White House as one of the most popular presidents in history. Rightly or wrongly, he was credited with bringing down the Berlin Wall and (in collaboration with Mikhail Gorbachev) ending the Cold War; of generating an economic boom and ending a painful national slide into recession, high inflation and suffocating interest rates while reviving Americans' pride in themselves.

There I was sitting in his living room, casually sipping coffee with Ronald and Nancy Reagan shortly after he left the White House, as if it was something I did every day, and it was very heady.

The agreement to collaborate on his autobiography was taken care of quickly. I bluffed my way through it having no idea what a ghostwriter was supposed to do but pretending I did.

Janklow said my name wouldn't appear on the cover of the book because it was to appear Reagan wrote the book himself. We agreed I'd spend several months tape recording his recollections, sometimes at his home but usually at his post-presidential office in the Fox Plaza building overlooking the 20th Century Fox movie studio in Los Angeles' Century City.

Once I had enough information, I would begin writing the book and show each set of new pages to Reagan, who would go over them and make additions or changes.

After agreeing to a schedule for the interviews, Reagan left with his Secret Service detail for a previously scheduled haircut, Janklow departed, and I was left sitting next to Nancy Reagan in their library. I found her likeable and, unsurprisingly, fiercely determined to protect Reagan's reputation.

"I get the impression," I'd said as we sat down, "that the President is not especially introspective."

"*He's not introspective at all.* Bob, you're going to have to really dig."

In other words, I thought, remembering the advice of my high school journalism teacher, I'd have to search hard to identify the essence of Reagan that would make his memoir authentic.

"Do you have any thoughts on what factors might have shaped him that might help?"

"When he was a little boy, he moved from one school to another year after year, his family was always moving. That must have had some effect on him." And of course, she added, his father had a problem with alcohol and that may also have had an effect.

She predicted I'd find Reagan erected a kind of emotional wall around him that many people, including even their children, found hard to penetrate.

"I noticed he doesn't seem to have much guile."

"*He doesn't have any guile.*"

She said she and "Ronnie" judged people differently: When the two of them walked into a room and met unfamiliar people, he assumed the best of them and was instinctively trustful while she was wary about their motives until proven otherwise.

I suggested we devote about a third of the book to Reagan's pre-presidential years, the balance to his presidency, and she agreed.

Within a few days I returned to Los Angeles and placed a tape recorder in front of Reagan at his desk in the Fox Plaza and started asking questions.

Right off the bat I made a mistake. After this first round of interviews, I'd hired a free lance typist in Monterey to transcribe the tape recordings but soon realized embarrassing remarks or even national security secrets might end up leaking to the tabloid press if I continued. Sandy volunteered to transcribe the tapes, beginning what we joked was a year and a half "mom and pop business."

Monday mornings I flew to Los Angeles, drove to Century City and was ushered into Reagan's office. After three or four hours, the tape recorder spinning between us, a catered lunch was wheeled into his office and we continued with the recorder shut off.

Sometimes Nancy joined us for lunch and I was surprised by how *ordinary* they could seem as a married couple.

Reagan loved sweets and almost every day Nancy had to rein in his desire for pie or ice cream. And in a wifely ritual I'd seen many times among friends--and in fact, at my own dinner table--Nancy would daub a little spit on her napkin, reach out and remove a breadcrumb or piece of salad from his cheek.

Despite what I'd read, Reagan didn't take orders from Nancy. At least until we reached the final stages of the project he seemed to get the last word when they disagreed, although he tried to placate her with compromises.

My biggest surprise during those first weeks was how emotionally committed Reagan was to ending the threat of nuclear war. I'd regarded him in the past as a kind of saber-rattling warmonger, in part because of his bellicose anti-Soviet rhetoric like describing the USSR as an "Evil Empire."

He said he hadn't been in office more than a few hours before he realized, after being briefed on the nuclear missile launch codes carried by a military aide who constantly shadowed him, how close the world was to mutual annihilation because the US and USSR each employed a strategy called "Mutual Assured Destruction." Each nation kept launch-ready enough nuclear-tipped ICBMs to survive a surprise attack and still be able to retaliate with enough nuclear firepower to destroy the other.

Because of this epiphany during his first moments in office, he said he became determined to somehow negotiate a way "out of this MAD-ness."

After the first couple of weeks, a rhythm set into my research. After four days of interviews I flew home to Carmel Thursday afternoons, give the latest tapes to Sandy and began writing.

I soon realized Nancy was right when she said I had to dig.

"I'm trying to write the memoirs of someone who doesn't have much memory, " I told Sandy after my third or fourth trip to Los Angeles.

She said she knew it from repeatedly typing Reagan's " I don't remember" replies to my questions that she'd been transcribing. When this happened, she said, I sometimes got impatient with Reagan and showed it: I'd pause after his answer, then rephrase my question repeatedly, sometimes too emphatically. When he became frustrated by the questioning, she said he began to tap the eraser of his pencil on my tape recorder, unable to come up with whatever answer I was seeking. She told me I should go easier on him.

Was Reagan beginning his descent into Alzheimer's Disease? It may have been, but I can't prove it.

He had vivid recollections of his school days, remembering the names of classmates on his high school and college football teams, details of his life as a radio announcer and film actor. But once we got into the presidential years he often had trouble remembering the details of relatively recent events or the identities of players in his administration.

Maybe his forgetfulness was partly by choice: He instructed me to be very selective in emphasizing the accomplishments of different individuals in the administration because he didn't want to hurt the feelings of others he didn't mention or praise. He declined to criticize virtually anyone except Secretary of State Alexander Haig, who he said came into the Oval Office demanding Reagan change his policies, and Chief of Staff Donald Regan who made the mistake of hanging up on Nancy.

In an oral history for the University of Virginia, Fred Ryan, Reagan's Los Angeles chief of staff, recalled the first days of preparing the autobiography:

One thing about President Reagan is he would probably be a very hard subject for you to interview because he was never introspective…I was in there for a lot of interviews with him. It was very hard to get him to talk about himself in terms of his Presidential policies…but he took it on [the autobiography]. Right up front he said, 'All right, I'll do it." He knew what he was getting into. It was hard for him to talk about himself. It was more the events. He would talk about the events that unfolded and how he saw himself in there, but there wasn't a lot of the stuff where he'd say, 'Well, here's what I was thinking at the time. It was more, 'This was said and so I said this,' and this is what I'd hoped we could do. But to do the book—I think he was relieved when it was over… It was a little hard at first because I think Lindsey thought the President was just going to sit and ramble on about himself, and then Lindsey would put it in biography form. It was a little more of a challenge to get him to talk about himself. So we'd take his calendars for each year and put those in front of him so he could recall what was happening on each of those days. He even had his diaries. He kept this handwritten diary, which was used for him to refresh his memory but was not put into his memoir. So he had a little bit of a challenge on that.

35

During my earliest trips to Los Angeles to meet with Reagan I stayed overnight with Steve. But with my afternoons free, I began driving to 12900 Mulholland Drive to visit Marlon, and he offered me the use of his guesthouse when I was in L.A.

Thus began a surreal chapter of my life.

Mornings and lunches were in the uptight, tightly controlled, Secret Service-protected, rigidly scheduled, coat and tie world of the presiding pope of political conservatism.

Afternoons, evenings and dinners were spent with another actor, an eccentric, lazy, paranoid wearing a kimono and fuzzy wuzzy slippers whose huge mastiff dog, *Tim*, climbed into my bed in the guesthouse at night despite my entreaties for him to sleep on the floor.

At first we continued taping interviews for the book about Clavell, who eventually succumbed to Marlon's legal assault and acknowledge legally that Petra was his daughter.

Christina cooked us dinner and afterward we'd spend an hour or two in his sauna, hot tub or swimming pool talking, a period in which we became close friends. Often these evenings were very long, and I wouldn't get to sleep until 2 am or so. The following morning I drank a lot of coffee before meeting with Reagan at 9 or 9:30 am.

I hadn't been bunking in the guesthouse long before Caroline, Marlon's assistant and Petra's mother, joined us in the living room and said she decided she didn't want a book written about the paternity battle because the publicity would be painful just as Petra was entering college.

A few days later, a UPS truck pulled up at our house in Carmel and took away the cartons of documents on Clavell. They had almost filled an entire room.

That would seem to end the need for our meetings, but Marlon said he wanted to continue our friendship. His long time best friend, Wally Cox, had died years before and he'd had a falling out with another close friend, film director George Englund, and he needed a pal.

I urged him to reconsider his decision not to write an autobiography but he was adamant. He hated discussing his movies, he said, and that's what publishers would want. Acting was the least interesting part of his life and besides, he wasn't going to pander to the public's curiosity about his sex life.

By now I had realized Christina was pregnant and more than Marlon's cook and maid.

An immigrant from Guatemala, Christina seemed smart and her interactions with Marlon suggested he deferred to her more than I would have expected. I guess proximity had brought them together.

Marlon bought her a $500,000 home with a swimming pool, tennis court and guesthouse not far from his compound, and she brought a large number of not-very-affluent relatives from Guatemala to join her, evoking visions in my mind (apologies to her family) of the "Beverly Hillbillies" moving into a mansion.

When one of her relatives--her father, I think--was having trouble legally entering the country, Marlon interrupted one of my visits to call the regional director of the Immigration and Naturalization Service in San Pedro who took the call when someone said "Marlon Brando is calling."

Whatever red tape had blocked the Guatemalan's entry was soon cut.

Marlon frequently called people out of the blue and immediately got through to them because of his name or voice, although "sometimes they just hang up on me because they don't believe I'm who I say I am."

During one of my visits he called the Palestinian activist, Hanan Ashrawi, to discuss what was holding up peace negotiations with Israel. Once he called Oprah Winfrey to talk about one of her interviews. Another day he told me that the night before he'd called the author Toni Morrison and told her:

"I want to make love to you. I want to rub my head into your breasts and rub my hands all over your body."

He didn't tell me what she replied.

36

I suppose every biographer, maybe foolishly, searches for a psychological turning point in his subject's evolution that turns his character in one direction or another--a "Rosebud" moment, as in Orson Wells' *Citizen Kane*.

Reagan said he couldn't think of any when I asked him, but he described an incident when he was about eleven years old that seemed important to him. As Nancy alerted me, he had had an especially insecure childhood because of frequent moves to new schools and his father's alcoholism. Moreover, he didn't see very well when he was young because, not yet realizing it, he needed glasses, causing him to do poorly in sports, which were important to him.

Before television or network radio, residents in many small towns assembled in schools or auditoriums for homegrown entertainment events called "readings." They stood up before their neighbors and spoke about whatever topic they wanted—a sonnet by Shakespeare, a poem they'd composed, maybe a reenactment of a scene from a famous play or movie.

After several weeks of coaxing by his mother, an amateur thespian, Reagan stood up, gave a reading and got a burst of applause whose intensity he remembered vividly more than half a century later.

"I really liked the sound of that," he told me.

For the first time, something he did brought him admiration and approval, and I suspect it may have helped set the course of a life in which he instinctively craved and sought approval from others and learned how to get it, first as a radio announcer, then as a movie actor, then a political spellbinder, finally as President.

During hours of interviews, despite my trying, he seldom evaluated events in an analytical way. It was not his thing. As Nancy said, his mind didn't work that way.

One example: A hallmark of the Reagan administration was long running conflict between Secretary of State George Schultz, who favored Reagan's effort to end the MAD doctrine and possibly eliminate nuclear weapons, and Secretary of Defense Caspar Weinberger, who, siding with some of his generals, opposed large cutbacks in the US nuclear arsenal because he believed the Soviets couldn't be trusted. But the two of them shared more than differences over foreign policy; Reagan aides told me the two cabinet officers strongly disliked each other.

I asked Reagan if he understood the roots of the bad blood.

"Maybe it went back to when they were both [working as executives at Bechtel. I don't know."

That was it. He didn't seem curious or contemplative about what the reasons might have been.

37

I was beginning to learn through on-the- job experience how a good ghostwriter should work, remembering what Bill Kamrath had told me in the 10th grade: To find the truth you have to work at it, search for it. By listening to and eliciting the thoughts of his subject the ghostwriter must learn to inhabit his mind, become his alter ego, impersonate him, think like him, write like him.

Millions of Americans knew how Reagan "sounded." After eight years of speeches by the 'Great Communicator" they recognized the cadence of his words, the rhythm of his sentences, the timing of his pauses, his tendency to start sentences *"Well...,"* I had to learn how to mimic that "voice."

I transferred his sentences from Sandy's transcripts directly into the manuscript when I could, but inevitably I had to write transitional paragraphs or other verbal bridges on my own, using language his readers recognized as authentic. Before we included these passages in the book, Reagan read them over to assure they said what he wanted to say. But once we got started, he virtually never changed anything I'd written.

Reagan's diary helped a lot. Each night when he was President he wrote a brief note about the day's events, and I used it to refresh his memory. It was an invaluable source in writing his autobiography.

The number of journalists and historians who have called Reagan "opaque" or hard to fathom is legion, Even his authorized biographer, Edmund Morris, who spent hours with him in the White

House, resorted to inventing a fictitious character to try to explain the mysteries of Reagan's personality and virtually gave up trying to do it.

I think Reagan was simple to explain:

"<u>What you see is what you get</u>."

Ever since he'd gone into politics, he said he knew critics mocked him because he was a former actor.

"People say how could you be President if you're an actor; well, I don't see how you could be President without being an actor!"

With warmth and Gary Cooper-like bashful, frequent nods of his head -- a technique he may have developed as an actor--he projected a contagious aura that made others want to protect him, as if somehow he had pumped a special gas into the air conditioner that made you like the guy.

William French Smith, his first attorney general, told me while I was researching an article during the 1980 campaign:

"*Ron has a secret weapon. He's likeable.*"

Rhetorically, I once told Sandy I liked him so much "I might kill for him."

I think some of his White House aides may have felt similarly and gotten Reagan into trouble during the Iran-Contra affair by deciding to help the Contra rebels in Nicaragua and exchanging weapons for hostages in Iran even though it was illegal, because that's what they thought he wanted.

While researching the book I read scores of analytical articles in which journalists--including some from the *New York Times*-- confidently accused Reagan of being manipulative, maybe even deceitful, during clashes with Congressional Democrats, saying one thing when intending something different, or that he did something "to protect his legacy." But when I read the minutes of Cabinet meetings, his diary and other documents to compare reality with these self-confident analysis, the pundits were almost always wrong. Reagan was what he appeared to be: What you saw is what you got.

Right or wrong, he had fundamental principles he followed unwaveringly: People were inherently good and deserved equal opportunities to better their lives and be protected from potential enemies by a strong national defense; America was exceptional, "a city on a hill," whose destiny was to champion freedom, democracy, free markets and the rule of law for all people.

He believed virtually anything government can do (except national defense) private enterprise can do cheaper and more efficiently; the way to slow the growth of government was to "starve the beast," reducing funding to bureaucrats so they must spend tax dollars more effectively; that Big Government and over regulation of business was corrosive to the human spirit because it squashed initiative and Communism was headed for the scrap heap because it stifled human enterprise. These were visceral, deep seated, instinctive principles to Reagan, consistent and non negotiable. As a ghostwriter all I had to do was master them and write the book using these values as he would write it. Because of his consistency it was easy to impersonate Reagan.

When he was President and warned Federal air traffic controllers he would fire them if they carried out a threatened strike because it was *illegal, I* knew he'd keep his word--and he did, probably undermining the US labor movement forever. During our interviews I mentioned economist Arthur Laffer had claimed credit for inventing "Reaganomics" or "supply side economics," the controversial doctrine asserting that lowering taxes unleashed economic growth, not stifled it. He quickly dismissed the notion. I don't think he even remembered who Laffer was. Its real origin, he said, was on a movie set, when he was making pictures and the maximum marginal personal Federal income tax rate exceeded 70 per cent. "I thought, why should I work for twenty or thirty per cent?" When he considered not working because of high taxes he realized 60 or 70 people on the movie set would lose their jobs. Lowering taxes, he said, increased incentive to work because people could keep more of what they earned and this would filter down through the economy.

He believed in political compromise. As president of the Screen Actors Guild, he said he'd learned it was "better to get 70 per cent of what you want than nothing" and that during negotiations it was prudent to give some ground to your opponent to avoid humiliating him.

Over lunch one day we talked about the *other* actor I'd been visiting. The two had something in common, I said. Besides being actors he and Brando both had fathers who were alcoholics. Reagan regarded Brando as a very good actor but seemed disgusted when I told him Marlon was now too lazy to memorize his lines and either wrote them on placards glued to a fellow actor or used an assistant (usually Caroline Barrett) who spoke his lines into a transmitter from the edge of the set he heard through an earpiece and repeated.

About six months into our interviews, opinion polls started to turn against the Reagans after they accepted an offer of more than $2 million from Japanese interests to make a kind of victory lap in Japan. Critics accused them of cashing in on his presidency.

Mark Weinberg, Reagan's press secretary, tried to explain why the Reagans were surprised and hurt by the negative publicity.

"They were celebrities almost their whole lives," he said. "In their world people get paid for making public appearances. It's normal."

In a phone call with Michael Korda, the Simon & Schuster editor in chief overlooking work on Reagan's memoirs, I said I was worried about the scandal's impact on book sales and his company's approximately $7 million investment..

"It's not our job to worry about that," he said.

After finishing one of my first sessions with Reagan, I heard on the radio that Marlon's son Christian had been arrested for killing Cheyenne's boy friend, Dag Drollet, at the Brando home on Mulholland Drive the previous night.

I called one of Marlon's private numbers and left a message of condolence and offered to do what I could do to help.

He returned my call four days later, tearful and despondent.

Cheyenne was seven or eight months pregnant with the child of Drollet, a member of a prominent Tahitian family, when he flew to Los Angeles to see her. On the evening of May 16, 1989, Christian told police he went to dinner with Cheyenne at a Hollywood restaurant and she claimed (lying perhaps) Drollet had been physically abusive to her. When they returned to the Brando home, Christian, now drunk, got into a fight with Drollet, pulled out an automatic pistol and shot him to death.

Marlon, who was in another part of the house, rushed into the room and applied mouth to mouth resuscitation too late to save Drollet and Christian was arrested for murder.

Brando told me his first impulse was to hire William Kunstler, a civil rights attorney whom he'd met while marching in a Martin Luther King rally to defend Christian. Kunstler persuaded him that he needed a criminal attorney and he contacted Robert Shapiro, who later would get national television time as one of O.J. Simpson's lawyers. Marlon said:

"Shapiro wants a million-dollars up front as a retainer," Marlon told me, "and he said, 'If you think I've done a good job, you can give me a bonus.'"

After the shooting, Marlon arranged for Cheyenne to fly to a clinic in Tahiti where she could get psychiatric help and keep her out of the reach of Ira Reiner, the Los Angeles District Attorney, whom he claimed was trying to ride Christian's arrest-- and his father's fame --to higher office.

38

With passage of time the Reagan presidency lost some of its luster. Huge deficits logged during his administration, deregulation of financial institutions that may have contributed to the Great Recession and questions about a foreign policy that included backing Saddam Hussein have arguably diminished his reputation. There may always be differences among presidential historians over exactly how much his policies contributed to ending the Cold War but from the perspective of his ghostwriter, I believe Reagan, whatever his flaws, helped reduce the threat of the global annihilation that haunted the world for decades and, not incidentally, brought down Soviet communism, largely because of his personal charm.

He told me early in his presidency it occurred to him:

"I wished I could get Brezhnev alone in a room the way I used to with Jack Warner and Louie B. Mayer, [and other studio heads when he was negotiating actors' contracts as president of the Screen Actors Guild], so we could try to work out things person to person."

There were four Soviet leaders while he was president, and he sent each a hand written letter suggesting that they meet in person. Until Gorbachev he got only rejections or silence . Besides ignoring his approach, "They kept dying on me," he joked.

After I was cleared by an FBI security team, I was permitted to enter a warehouse in Southern California that stored millions of documents generated during the Reagan administration and were being prepared to be moved to the still unfinished Reagan Presidential Library.

I was searching for his correspondence with the Soviet leaders. An archivist wearing protective gloves brought out the files I requested and offered me matching gloves. Reagan's opening letters to each of the four Soviet leaders were frank and candid, comparing the Soviet system critically with that of the United States, but containing a hint of conciliation, arguing it was time for the two sides to attempt to defuse the nuclear powder keg that could easily destroy both countries and exterminate hundreds of millions of people.

Gorbachev, like his predecessors, initially responded that he didn't trust Reagan or the United States enough to accept his proposal for a summit conference.

Reagan kept writing, usually in longhand, and was shocked by the replies, he told me, because they made him realize that Kremlin leaders actually feared the United States might launch a preemptive nuclear strike. He said he became committed to convincing the Russians otherwise.

Eventually Gorbachev warily accepted Reagan's proposal for a summit and agreed to meet in Geneva. Reagan arranged for the two of them to meet privately in front of a blazing fireplace in a lakefront cottage with only their interpreters so they could talk "grandfather to grandfather…probably the only two men in the world who could bring about World War III. "

After Geneva, the letters continued. As I held them in my hand and read the back and forth exchange of messages over three or four years I saw the exchanges become more cordial, less mistrustful; hostility and mistrust begin to evolve over time into a genuine, eventually even warm relationship between the two men. These letters were the raw materials of a monumental change in history, and when I held them in my hands and read them it was as if I was watching the world become a safer place, and it was thrilling.

I think Reagan's charm and personality, first transmitted in his letters, then the person to person meetings with Gorbachev, were the instruments that would start the thaw in the long Cold War-- although his commitment to an unprecedented peacetime military arms buildup that the Russians couldn't afford to match (including the ill conceived but threatening "Star Wars" missile defense system) were also factors, as were his oratory, with his challenge in Berlin: "Mr. Gorbachev, tear down this wall!"

Reagan told me he thought Gorbachev believed Communism would survive the reforms he was introducing in the Soviet Union-- Glasnost and Perestroika—largely because the arms control agreements he was negotiating with Reagan would drastically cut Soviet spending on arms and give it more resources for improving his nation's economy. But Reagan said he never doubted that once Gorbachev granted a little freedom to his citizens and unleashed his reforms the Russian public wouldn't let him stop.

The final act in preparing Reagan's autobiography for publication was played out over a long conference table at his post-presidential offices. His lawyers, George Schultz and the National Security Council had already vetted the manuscript for errors, improper disclosure of classified materials or verbal landmines that could cause Reagan trouble in the ongoing Iran-Contra hearings Reagan sat at the head of the table with me on one side and Nancy on the other, joined by Chief of Staff Fred Ryan and a rotating group of staff aides. We spent most of five days going over the book a page at a time, sometimes reading passages aloud. Nancy was alert for anything that might distract from her vision of Reagan as a statesman and blue-penciled a few passages including the reference to Reagan's desire early in his administration to get Leonid Brezhnev in a room alone--as he had with the studio heads when he was president of the Screen Actors Guild--to see if the two of them could begin to work out an arms agreement. She thought the reference to studio bosses would remind readers too much that Ronnie was originally an actor.

Reagan gave in, as he did with most cuts Nancy or the staff suggested. But he refused her emphatic appeal to retain passages I'd written (after she encouraged it) criticizing Marine Col. Oliver North, the White House aide whose less than honest representations made him a key figure in the Iran-Contra affair. Because of his military background, I suspect, Reagan regarded him as something of a hero and penciled out criticism of North, to Nancy's disappointment.

Before each of our luncheon recesses during this final burst of editing Nancy usually cornered me and said she needed my help persuading Reagan to remove different passages she was concerned about -- for example, a section in which he strongly criticized the press for becoming blood thirsty sharks whenever a politician was wounded by a setback.

If I didn't do what she'd asked, she shook my knee vigorously but silently under the tablecloth to remind me of her request. I continued to be her ally for several days and did what she asked but one day just before lunch I said: "You know, he was President for eight years and I think we have to go along with his opinions."

In return I got a cold hard stare. I don't think our relationship was ever as warm as it was previously.

Still, I gained respect for Nancy Reagan. Not only did she do whatever she could to protect her husband—a trait any husband would value—as First Lady she'd had to survive a wave of attacks by her husband's political enemies when they were unable to score hits on the Teflon President. She was also a lot more vulnerable than I'd expected..

During one morning I spent with the Reagans in their Bel Air home, she repeatedly broke into tears as first she recalled being told that she should have a mastectomy and said she feared her husband would find her less attractive; she was in tears again a few minutes later when she recalled the political bullets fired at her because she'd borrowed designer clothes from haut couture houses and accepted new White House china from political supporters.

She was reputed to be a tough cookie, and I guess she was, but she had a tender, less apparent side that few of her critics acknowledged. .

Over the nearly two years I worked for Reagan he sent me several notes and photographs signed "Your friend, Ron." He may have meant it, but I think he really had only one friend, Nancy.

Ronald Reagan: An American Life" was published in October, 1990 to generally favorable but some negative reviews and it made best seller lists in several countries..

On November 25, Reagan sent me a handwritten note:

Dear Bob:

I'm ashamed of myself for not writing this sooner. The book is out, finished and a success and very largely due to you. I couldn't have done it without you and I'm eternally grateful.

It was great working with you, an experience I'll always remember, especially those days across the desk from each other with the tape machine running. A lot of people have gone out of the way to praise me for the book and every time it happens I say a silent thank you to a fellow named Robert Lindsey.

Again my heartfelt thanks and God Bless you. Nancy joins me in this.

Sincerely, Ron.

39

\

While I was finishing my work with President Reagan, Carol Matthau still called often to talk about her troubles, her children, Truman Capote's alcoholic spiral or Johnny Carson's marriages or whatever topics occupied her thoughts that day, but also to report on her latest research regarding Admiral Canaris. She was as determined as ever to prove the decency of "one good German" and pleased that the recent publication of previously classified MI6 documents that seemed to support although not prove her hypothesis that the German admiral may have secretly collaborated with Britain during the war before Hitler ordered his execution..

She said Marlon hadn't returned her calls for weeks and asked me to ask him why he'd ignored them. Until the shooting at Marlon's home, they'd talked every night via the secret phone hidden under her bed.

When I asked him about it, he said that as far as he was concerned, Carol no longer existed. Almost alone among his friends, she hadn't called or sent a note after the shooting and he could not forgive her.

Carol was shattered. She said she hadn't wanted to bother him during the crisis and asked me to explain this to him.

During the next few months I took her request to Marlon countless times, telling him she was terribly hurt and explaining why she hadn't called. I said she was an old friend and he owed her forgiveness. Marlon never spoke to her again.

Meanwhile his anger zeroed in on another target, District Attorney Reiner.

"This is not the Christian Brando case," he said during a rare encounter with reporters after one of Christian's court hearings *"This is the Marlon Brando case."*

He claimed that prosecutors-- if their defendant's father hadn't been famous--would have normally proposed a plea bargain charging Christian with manslaughter.

For weeks he rarely spoke of anything except his desire to get revenge on the prosecutors. Neither his charm nor his celebrity stopped the prosecutors, although in the end Marlon won the battle by default with a strategic move.

To get a murder conviction, prosecutors believed they needed Cheyenne's testimony. But Marlon had sent her to the psychiatric clinic in Tahiti and repeated moves by the District Attorney's office to persuade a judge to make her return to California failed. Christian ultimately pleaded guilty to manslaughter and was sentenced to a state prison at San Luis Obispo, California.

Marlon made several unannounced back-gate visits to the penitentiary arranged by sympathetic prison officials to enable him to avoid waiting paparazzi.

Christian would spend five years at the prison protected from other, predatory prisoners by a rotating phalanx of American Indians, a spontaneous gesture of gratitude for Marlon's support of Native Americans, a gesture that brought tears to his eyes every time he mentioned it.

40

After Oona O'Neil, one of Carol Matthau's best friends, died at 66 in 1991, Carol told me Oona visited her every night at the foot of her bed, and they chatted about their lives and loves and friendship, her marriages to Saroyan, Oona's love for Chaplin and the painful rejection by her father as well as Carol's love for Walter and their son, Charlie.

Carol quoted her conversations with her dead friend to me word for word. I didn't know what to say, so I just listened.

She never got over Marlon's rebuff and for years continued to press me to persuade him to call her.

In 1992, she published an autobiography, *Among the Porcupines*, that was well received by critics, and she sent us a copy of the book along with a letter:

Dear Bob and Sandra, the best friends in the world.

I think of you both often and the way you live and all that you are. I'm so grateful to know you...

It's an awful book.. Not the one I started and finished. But in my usual daze I let it happen like this. I sent one to Marlon, thanking him, but I know he'll hate it (and he'll be right)...I don't know where I'm going next, New York or Connecticut. I'll let you know when I decide. I'm about finished with [the book about] Canaris...to use a disgusting phrase, it's 'in depth,' if anything is. It is called '*The Quest for Canaris.*' I'll call you to tell you that nothing is happening and to tell you to please make a small sphere for me in your life. You are almost my last friend. Everyone else I love has died.

I love you.

Carol

Several years later Carol telephoned and said she hadn't been feeling well and felt unable to complete the Canaris book after all and asked me to finish it for her using her research materials. I'd encouraged her for years to write the book, and I'm sure she believed I'd take it over. When I told her I didn't think I had the time to do it, she was surprised and hurt and I don't think she ever forgave me completely.

After Walter died in 2000, Carol continued to call   from hotels in New York , Chicago and elsewhere and often mentioned that her health was declining.

At the age of 78, she died July 20, 2003 in New York City of a brain aneurism, the Canaris book unfinished.

PART THREE

41

As I mentioned at the beginning of this memoir, Sandy and I were hosting six friends at a Saturday night dinner party when Marlon called and I told him I'd call him back later, and he began sobbing. This is what he'd said:

Someone he knew, someone very famous, *a thirty-five year old man*-- had just left Marlon's home after telling him that he had "married" an eleven year-old boy that morning, that he had given him a wedding ring and was in love with the child.

Marlon said he suspected the relationship might be sexual.

He didn't know what to do, who to tell.
'What would you do?"

As I hung up and returned to our guests I realized immediately whom he was talking about.

He'd told me several days before Michael Jackson was coming to his home for acting lessons because Jackson was determined to become a film star. Marlon's son Miko worked for Jackson as one of his bodyguards and he'd offered to give him some lessons on acting.

When I called Marlon back after our guests left, I said it was obvious he was describing Michael Jackson. He made me promise not to reveal what he'd said, and I haven't until now.

Of course, I didn't have evidence or proof if what Jackson (or Marlon) said was *true*. It seemed fantastical. But I kept this secret, ignoring whatever obligation I had as a journalist or a citizen. Almost two years later, the police would raid Jackson's estate, *Neverland Ranch*, and Jackson would be accused of molesting a prepubescent boy.

During the previous intervening months I'd known of the likelihood that the world's most famous rock star may have had a bizarre relationship with an eleven year old boy. For a (former) reporter it was an enormous and painful scoop to sit on, but because of my promise to Marlon I didn't say anything about it except to a few friends, although as I will explain, Marlon and I did our best to stop Jackson, even tried blackmailing him.

Still upset and tearful when I returned his call just before midnight, Marlon said Jackson had mentioned his "marriage" during the acting lesson when Marlon asked him to replicate an emotional episode from his life as part of the instruction.

He said he didn't know who else to turn to, I was the only person he knew who'd been sexually molested as child. What should he do?

I said I had no idea. I wasn't an expert on child abuse but said I imagined the emotional impact on the child—even more so because of Jackson's fame-- could be overwhelming and last a lifetime.

When we spoke the next day, Marlon asked me again to promise not to mention to anyone what he'd said the night before.

We decided on three possibilities to respond to Jackson's admission of his "marriage:" Tell the police, arrange psychiatric help for Jackson, or try to persuade him to stop.

I called a former Palos Verdes neighbor, Dr. Albert Silver, who had a psychiatry practice in Beverly Hills, and said Marlon Brando knew a well known singer who'd admitted molesting children, and would he be able to treat such a patient? Could you speak to him hypothetically? He agreed to talk to Marlon, but their conversation was brief: if a patient admitted sexually molesting a child, Silver said he was legally required to report him to child welfare authorities.

Marlon was still almost pathologically outraged over Los Angeles authorities' handling of Christian's case, and he refused to consider reporting Jackson to the authorities. (Also I don't think it was in his character to be a "snitch.")

Jackson's security staff at *Neverland* included at least one former Los Angeles policeman, and Marlon suggested we ask him for advice, then retracted the suggestion after I said if the ex-cop was on Jackson's payroll, he was unlikely to do anything to put him in jail and give up his meal ticket.

That's when we came up with the idea of trying to blackmail Jackson by getting him to admit on film he'd molested the boy, then threaten to make it public unless he stopped.

Marlon was a gadgeteer, owner of a multitude of recording devices and home television equipment stored in a building on his property he called "the bunker."

The scheme we agreed on was to conceal a camera atop a cabinet in Marlon's living room and connect it to a video cassette recorder, then Marlon would coax Jackson into repealing his story about the child and we'd have our evidence.

We spoke on the phone about an hour before Jackson was due for a visit, and our stage was ready.

A couple of hours later Marlon called me and I asked anxiously:

"How'd it go?"

Marlon said that he'd had no trouble getting Jackson to talk about the child again and, amazingly, Jackson didn't think he'd done anything wrong in "marrying" the child. He seemed to regard himself as a child who was simply dealing with a peer.

"Did you get it on tape?"

Marlon paused a long moment, then admitted he had pressed the wrong buttons when he programmed the VCR, so it hadn't recorded the conversation.

We agreed to try again in two or three weeks when Jackson was due at Marlon's home again.

This time we decided I'd be wired into the conversation so I could coach Marlon if necessary. Besides setting up the same video camera, he wore the radio earpiece he used when Caroline Barrett fed him lines from a script offstage on a movie set, and it was connected to me via a cell phone that he put on a coffee table near Jackson so I could hear the conversation.

In Carmel, I waited with our phone line open at the appointed time but I heard only silence, making me think something had gone wrong again.

Finally, after hearing what sounded like Marlon's deep voice, I said:

"*What'd you say?*"

Unfortunately, Marlon explained later, my words boomed so loudly out of the tiny cell phone that Jackson instinctively looked up and scanned the room searching for the source of the voice.

Marlon quickly invited him to another room to show him something (I don't remember what) to deflect his attention, and that ended our electronic scheme to blackmail Jackson.

Our next move was for Marlon to invite himself to *Neverland*, Jackson's 2,700 acre spread north of Santa Barbara filled with realizations of his Peter Pan fantasies come to life: a railroad, amusement park, Ferris wheel, zoo, a replica of Disneyland's Main Street, statues and monuments to the ageless Peter Pan, the child who never grew up.

When he returned, Marlon said he'd seen several young boys seemingly unattached to parents partying on Jackson's amusement rides and entering Jackson's home. When he inquired who they were several Jackson employees told him there were always prepubescent boys at *Neverland*.

At *Neverland* and during his next acting lesson, Marlon said Jackson spoke again about the eleven year old and according to Marlon, said he'd never had sexual relations with anybody—male or female.

Marlon said he spent hours coaching Jackson to like girls, trying to persuade him to start dating and eventually get married.

A few months later, Jackson appeared to take Marlon's advice when he married Lisa Marie Presley, Elvis' daughter. We were pleased with ourselves. We thought we'd solved the problem, hit a homerun. We were wrong. It was apparently a loveless marriage that ended less than two years later.

42

Over dinner the first time Marlon met Sandy, I witnessed the force of his magnetism with women. We were at a restaurant in the San Fernando Valley and he was sitting next to Sandy. Leaving me to study my menu, Marlon stroked her wrist, looked into her eyes and asked her questions she later said made her feel as if she was the only woman on the planet.

Here was a man weighing at least 300 pounds whose famous good looks were long past their peak, and Sandy was mesmerized.

The next day he told me he thought Sandy was terrific.

"I think I'll steal her from you."

I didn't say anything.

I knew he had a history of doing exactly that to his friends.

There was a long pause.

"No," he said. "I'm kidding."

Still, I wondered what would have happened if he'd been serious.

Sandy and I were in Pittsburgh visiting Susan and her family when I checked my answering machine and found three messages from Marlon left during the previous two days.

When I called him back he said he was upset I hadn't returned his calls sooner. He'd figured from the number of rings before my machine activated that I must have ignored at least one of his calls. He liked to be in charge. I didn't always let him get away with it.

He said his friend George Englund had negotiated a deal with Harry Evans, the Publisher of Random House, for Marlon to write his autobiography but Englund wanted too much money to help him write it. If I'd do it, he'd pay me half what Englund wanted. I said I'd take it.

I knew he needed money but the decision to write a memoir shocked me. He had an annual income of close to $1 million from residuals, a Screen Actors Guild pension and back end payments of previous work. But he spent more than that, not only on Christian's legal expenses, but supporting his other children, taxes, keeping up his property on Mulholland Drive, Christina's home and his Tahitian atoll, Tetiaroa, where he suspected profits from his modest hotel were being skimmed by employees. He was not broke but most of his assets were tied up in real estate.

Although he still hated making movies for a few days' work he could earn almost $4 million and agreed to make a couple of bombs, *Christopher Columbus: The Discovery* and later *The Island of Dr. Moreau,* to keep solvent.

In his call to Pittsburgh he said he'd been promised $5 million by Evans to write an autobiography and he wouldn't have to put a lot of work into it because I'd be writing it. (He didn't tell me he had tried writing the book himself, had gotten nowhere and was months behind in meeting his deadline.)

He said his memoir would be useful to his children who knew him only from what they read in the tabloids, ignoring his previous stubborn, religious-like vow never to write an autobiography because it was unseemly and vulgar.

"I want to prove I can completely open up and talk about *anything.*"

Almost immediately, he added he wasn't going to write about *everything.*

His marriages, his wives and especially his children were off limits.

Before we could sign a contract, Marlon and I needed physical exams to establish we were healthy enough to take on the expensive project. I passed my exam with no problems; Marlon, who was then almost 70, had the beginnings of diabetes and weighed in at 305 pounds, and Random House made him take out an insurance policy with a premium of $304,645 to ensure its investment.

The publisher sent Marlon a check for $800,000, the first installment on the $5 million contract and promised the balance in installments as each third of the book was finished.

Marlon urged me to get started right away: the sooner I did, the sooner he'd get another check.

I began taping his recollections and Sandy transcribed them, our mom and pop shop reopened. I spent the next four or five weeks either at Marlon's home with my tape recorder, sharing a bed with *Tim* or at my computer at home, hurriedly assembling the beginnings of Marlon's memoir, focusing initially on his childhood and his toxic relationship with his father, a coarse, tough-guy alcoholic who Marlon said never did anything except drink, chase women on his rounds as a traveling salesman, and demean anything Marlon did as a child or teenager.

Because of his father's cruelty, Marlon said he'd had a lifelong contempt for authority and rebelled against anyone who tried to impose their will on him.

His mother, Dodie, was also an alcoholic who turned raising Marlon over to an olive skinned nanny called Ermi, the love of Marlon's life until she broke his heart by giving up her job to get married when he was about seven. For the rest of his life, he said he constantly chased brown skinned women, searching for the woman he lost as a child, but never able to trust any of them because he was afraid they would abandon him eventually.

Before long getting him to collaborate on the book was like trying to wrestle a greased pig. Once I'd written about 50,000 words and finished an outline for the balance of the book, Random House paid him about $1 million, bringing the total to almost $2 million. After the check was in the bank Marlon said he didn't want to work on the book for awhile because he didn't need any money. I was soon at a point where I couldn't write anymore because I needed more of Marlon's memories to proceed, and he refused to sit still and be interviewed.

During this pause--which lasted nearly three months--he said he wanted to visit me in Carmel to see how I lived.

He and I flew from Burbank in Southern California to San Jose and drove to Carmel. At the Burbank airport, I asked him to wait while I returned my rental car to the Avis lot.

"Why don't you just leave it there?," he said, pointing to the curb in front of the terminal.

He was serious: Why follow convention and tell the rental agency you've returned its car? He waited as I returned the car.

Sandy and I took Marlon to dinner at a favorite restaurant in Carmel where he signed autographs, was pleasant and entertained waiters and diners by sticking two breadsticks in his nostrils and pretending to be a walrus.

Mostly, Marlon said, he just wanted to hang out, and the two of us watched movies for hours in our family room. When we ordered take out in L.A., he often requested angel hair pasta with marinara sauce, and Sandy and I served it to him for lunch along with one of our most precious bottles of red wine. He didn't drink a drop, so my efforts to put on the dog with an expensive wine were wasted. I'd forgotten he didn't drink much.

After lunch Marlon looked out a window in our house and saw one rain gutter and downspout were disconnected and drooping downward and asked if I had a ladder.

I found one and he climbed to the top, his huge body cloaked in special-order, custom made, oversized jeans, and he reached up and reattached the gutter.

Sandy and I enjoyed the sight.

"Why don't you take a picture?," she asked.

I didn't because I knew that if he saw me with a camera he'd think I thought of him as a celebrity and I suspect that if I'd taken the picture our friendship would have been over. He just wanted to be "regular" friends. That's why I never asked him to autograph a picture--but often wished I'd taken a picture of him climbing the ladder to fix the gutter.

"I like to do things like that," he said after stepping off the ladder, looking up to take a last look at his handiwork.

When he got out of bed the next morning, I made coffee and he told me he'd had a dream the night before:

"I was in your living room and all your friends were here, and they were all talking about how fat I was."

43

By August, 1993 Marlon was running out of cash again and I was back at his home recording more memories when two friends of his son Miko who were employed by Michael Jackson came to the house looking stunned.

Policemen had raided *Neverland* that morning looking for evidence of child abuse, and the two Jackson employees wanted to discuss it because Miko said they could trust Marlon to give them good advice.

"Let's get out of here," he said, because he suspected his house might be bugged.

"You can say anything in front of him," he told them, referring to me as we got in the car. I sat in the back next to one of Jackson's employees.

Marlon took the driver's seat in the top of the line Mercedes the man and woman from *Neverland* arrived in, and for more than an hour we drove past the baronial homes of Beverly Hills talking about Jackson, as they named seven or eight or nine boys who had spent the night at *Neverland* in Jackson's bed. I don't remember all the names now, just a few on a long list that included many boys' popular names of that generation—Billy, Jimmy, Scott, Jordie…and others.

Jackson's employees said Jackson had an apartment on Wilshire Boulevard they called "the hideout," with a safe containing what I gathered were incriminating pictures of young boys but they hoped a private detective hired by Jackson had already been there that morning and emptied the safe. It turned out he had. But the police were swarming all over *Neverland* with search warrants and they didn't know what they'd find.

It was on this day I first observed a switch in Marlon's attitude regarding Jackson.

As we drove through the lush neighborhoods, the hours we'd spent discussing the emotional devastation heaped on molested children seemed to have been washed away, and he advised the two of them to stay away from *Neverland* and leave the area to avoid being questioned by the police.

Months later, Marlon was called to testify before a Grand Jury regarding his friendship with Jackson. I never learned exactly what he said, but when we spoke later on the day of his testimony, it was evident he had not mentioned the "marriage" ceremony or Jackson's other admissions.

"I didn't do him any harm," he said.

Several months later, prosecutors gave up their efforts to prosecute Jackson after their principal witness --a 13 year old boy -- refused to testify against him- after and he, his family and his lawyers received a payment totaling about $22 million from Jackson and his insurance company. I suspect—but don't know—that this was the same child Jackson had "married."

44

Shortly after his visit to Carmel, Marlon said he would never make another movie:

"I've decided to become a billionaire!"

It was not an unusual comment for Marlon, who often piped up with weird pronouncements that were a blend of hubris and naiveté.

He said he'd recently read an article about how many billionaires there were in the world, and all he needed was a good product to sell to become one. He asked me to go into business with him, using his fame as a hook and we would both become rich.

That's when we began making plans for *"Tahiti Rain."*

The rain that falls in French Polynesia, Marlon said, was the purest, best tasting water in the world, and he wanted to bottle it.

We'd collect the rainfall in huge tarpaulins, reservoirs or cisterns on his atoll or on the slopes of the Tahitian highlands, pump it to a staging area using solar power, store it, bottle it as *Marlon Brando's Tahiti Rain* and ship it to markets all over the world with his likeness on the label wearing the brimmed fedora he wore as a Mafia don in *The Godfather*. He'd done research on the Internet and learned bottled water was a fast growing, multi-billion dollar business, and he wanted to get in on it. If I'd help him start the business he'd give me

10 per of the earnings, perhaps more if it really took off, and he seemed to have no doubt it would.

Thus began a partnership we called *Frangipani*, named for a beautiful flower.

Over hours and hours I learned as much as I could about the bottled water business and discovered Marlon was right about its rapid growth, led by a few giants such as Perrier, Evian and San Pellegrino. I found out the U.S. Department of Agriculture had funded an obscure, successful experiment it called "water harvesting," to collect rainwater on huge sheets of canvas or plastic and that primitive forms of water harvesting had occurred in countless cultures going back centuries.

As I listened on an extension, Marlon interrogated an old friend, Paul Newman, about his salad dressing enterprise, and he said that if Marlon decided to produce a consumer product he should be sure it was among the best available in its category. We spent hours working out alternative and hypothetical scenarios in which we compared the economic merits of bottling the water in Tahiti or chartering ocean going tankers and shipping it in bulk to bottling lines in America. We scoured the country looking for old bottling plants we could buy anonymously and convert to our needs.

There are so many things we didn't think about…such as how, if we used Marlon's island as the source of our rainwater, we'd get the water off the island when it was virtually completely encircled by dangerous reefs? How would we keep *Tahiti Rain* healthy and uncontaminated while it was in transit to the US? What would Tahitian regulatory and taxing authorities think of the idea? Was it even practical to harvest surface water rather than pump it from aquifers, which all the big bottled water companies did?

Still we pushed ahead and decided we needed a partner already established in the bottled water business.

At the time one of the hotter plays on the stock market was a company called Clearly Canadian Beverage Corporation which was selling about $150 million a year worth of vitamin-enhanced water in distinctive blue bottles. We'd found our target.

Marlon, of course, was our front man. He called the company in Vancouver and once a secretary recognized his voice, he was quickly connected to Douglas Mason, the CEO.

Marlon said he wanted to discuss a business proposition but the company had to agree to keep his proposal secret. Lawyers worked out a confidentiality agreement that stated "Tahiti, S.A.. [Frangipani] is engaged in the development of a proprietary product for the bottled water market...Clearly Canadian understands and acknowledges that Confidential Information has been developed or obtained by Tahiti, S.A. by the investment of significant time, effort and expense and that the Confidential Information is a valuable, special and unique asset...which provides Tahiti, S.A. with a significant competitive advantage."

A couple of weeks later, Doug Mason arrived at Marlon's home with his wife, Carla.

Marlon showed him a sample of the label he'd designed for *Tahiti Rain,* his head bobbing out of the sea topped by his *Godfather* hat. Drinks were served and snapshots taken, although Marlon refused Mason's request to wear a baseball cap with a Clearly Canadian logo. Then Mason and his wife; Sandy and I and Marlon and Caroline Barrett went for dinner at a French restaurant on Ventura Boulevard in Sherman Oaks where we were the only customers in a huge room with no other tables. Marlon, who exchanged greetings with the owner in French, had asked him to close the area to other diners.

I didn't know if Mason responded to Marlon's call out of curiosity after hearing from a famous film star--a likely possibility--or whether he thought there might be merit in our idea.

For Marlon, it was an expensive evening; the bill for dinner was over $2,500, largely because of several expensive French wines selected by Mason.

Mason didn't challenge our concept of harvesting Tahitian rainwater but said he foresaw the biggest growth in the bottled water business in products enhanced with nutritional additives, responding to health conscious consumers. He was thinking of establishing a new health based product using Marlon's name.

And thus began what we all agreed was a secret project called "Project 99."

In a follow up fax, Mason wrote:

"Thank you so much for your hospitality on Carla's and my recent visit. We both felt very good about our brief stay. I wanted to make it absolutely clear that my enthusiasm for your rainwater project is intense despite my rambling on about my concepts for the beverage world future. I did that partly in answer to Bob's questions to me and partly out of my own conviction and vision for future Clearly Canadian projects. I didn't want you to think I was steering you in my vision's direction at the sacrifice of full investigation."

Indeed, he said, he'd already assigned his research department to explore producing *Tahiti Rain* as well as a possible alternative beverage. "Your ideas, endorsement and smiling face combined with our marketing and distribution would create a formidable team."

We thought *Tahiti Rain*--aka *Project 99*-- was on its way.

For awhile it was.

Mentally I started deciding how I'd spend my ten per cent of the profits, and Marlon asked me to determine which regions of the world had the highest annual rainfall so we could begin expanding beyond Tahiti. I dug into research on climate and rainfall. Meanwhile, Marlon talked to politicians he knew in Tahiti about his dream.

If Marlon was the front man, I was the bean counter.

Over the next three months, I exchanged more than forty letters and faxes with Mason and his legal and technical staffs. Marlon's lawyers billed thousands of dollars for drafting a contract.

Finally a fax arrived from Clearly Canadian with an offer of $1 million. "Soon we'll decide on the type of beverage you'll want to partner with us," Mason said. "I've got some exciting ideas I think you'll love."

In addition to the million-dollar signing bonus, Clearly Canadian offered a royalty for each case of the beverage that would be sold under Marlon's label, using a sliding scale that brought the royalty to as much as 25 cents a case.

I felt rich.

I called Marlon and said we'd closed the deal.

"How much?"

"A million."

"A million a year?"
"No, a million at signing, plus a percentage of what they sell."

He told me to send a reply demanding $1 *million every year guaranteed*.

I did, and I never got a reply; we never heard again from Clearly Canadian .

My $100,000 was out the window.

Curiously, Marlon may have been ahead of his time. Two years after our negotiations with Clearly Canadian collapsed. a new company began importing drinking water from the Fiji Islands in the South Pacific and found a substantial market in the United States. The difference was Fiji Water wasn't "harvesting" surface rainwater but pumping it from underground aquifers. In retrospect, we should have done the same thing.

Why worry?, Marlon asked when I lamented the rupture in our negotiations with Clearly Canadian. He said he had a new idea to realize his plan to become a billionaire: he'd sell DVDs on the Internet.

It was a couple of years before we could put that project together.

45

By early 1994, when I was close to finishing the book and Marlon had pocketed almost $4 million from Random House, he said he'd decided we should stop work on the manuscript and abandon it and keep the money we'd already been paid.

"Don't work on it anymore."

He said we could probably extort additional cash from Random House because it had already invested so much on the project it wouldn't risk losing its investment and we could ask for almost anything we wanted to finish the manuscript.

He said he'd learned how to get his way with directors and producers the same way: At the beginning of a new movie shoot, he followed directions no matter what he thought of them, until so much money had been spent on a movie that producers were in too deep to abandon it. Then they *had* to meet Marlon's demands. That's what he'd done, for example, while making the Vietnam movie *Apocalypse Now*. He had a different vision for portraying his character, Col. Walter Kurtz, than did director Francis Ford Coppola.

Initially, he played along with Coppola, then to get his way and force the director and producers to pay him more, he started purposefully forgetting his lines, making missteps on film, acting out of character, adding days to the costly production in the Philippines . He not only got more money—over a million dollars more—he forced Coppola to shape the movie the way Marlon wanted.

"This isn't the same thing," I said. "Publishers don't work that way."

We'd signed a contract, I said, and if we didn't complete the book as promised Random House would sue us and we'd have to return all the money it had paid us, plus probably a lot more. Besides, it was unethical and I wouldn't do it.

He insisted.

I said I wouldn't be part of his plan and hung up.

For weeks we stopped speaking while I plowed ahead on the manuscript with as much information as I already had, a compendium of recollections about his stage and film roles, some how-to observations about acting, more history of the psychic pain of his childhood and his hatred of his father, tales about a few of his hundreds of romantic conquests and a chapter about American Indians that brought him to tears when he read it.

When he needed more money, he called and said he was ready to work on the book again.

Before he'd halted the interviews, he'd repeatedly said he didn't want to write anything about his movies because they were the least important element of his life. He'd write about acting techniques but not individual movies. Instead of movies, he preferred to discuss the Israeli-Palestinian dispute, for example, or advances in biology or astrophysics, anything that was more interesting that Hollywood fantasies. Acting was a shallow, meaningless way for a man to spend his life, he said.

I insisted we had to write about his movies because it was the only reason people would pay $25 for his book or Random House would pay us $5 million to write it. Already his refusal to mention his wives and children made it an unusual memoir. At last I persuaded Marlon to answer a few more questions, and I finished the manuscript.

As I've mentioned, like any biographer, as I had with Reagan, I tried to search for events that suggested important turning points in his subject's life.

During one conversation, Marlon said he suspected that during his frustrating battle with prosecutors over Christian he'd learned he couldn't always get his way and as a result he may have lost some of the explosive, hair trigger sense of rage that had been part of him since high school.

Even though Marlon had repeatedly told me he didn't want even to allude to his wives or children in the book I wrote a line based on what he'd said, trying to make a subtle point:

"Over the last three years I've learned I'm not able to control everything in my life, so maybe it's changed me a bit," implying that during the long months dealing with Christian's problems he had mellowed.

Sandy and I were in Las Vegas when I heard the following message on our answering machine from Marlon after he had read a draft of the book containing this passage:

"If you don't change that Bob, you're going to know what it's like to feel real pain. I don't care about my own pain, but I do care about Christian's, and this is not an admonition that is intended to be gentle. This is a warning. I really don't think that you fully understand the potential of your anguish and the anguish of your wife that will result of a frontal, unstopping assault on you personally in public and there's more than one way to approach this, so you have to know. You have to be on your guard...you danced over the chalk line and you have to dance back. You have to fix it. Otherwise, your children, your wife and your friends are all going to know things they never would have guessed, and I'm talented. I spent my whole life fighting and knowing how to be a warrior. Don't think it's dead, Bob, and don't think I'm going to lie down...I won't let you up once you're down. I'll just keep pursuing you. Keep it in mind, Bob, because I swear on my kids that if you let this go by, the quality of your life isn't going to be worth a nickel."

He also left a second message on the answering machine:

If the passage wasn't eliminated from the book, he said he would inform the world "Your father made you suck his cock."

Of course, the irony of his calls was that they proved I was wrong in the first place to imply he'd changed: he was as capable of rage as ever .

Understandably, Sandy was as upset as I was. When we returned home, I sent a fax to Marlon's lawyer, Belinda Frixou, in London, with a transcript of his messages and added:

What's puzzling about his outburst is that Marlon previously edited and rewrote the passage he referred to on Page 559, making it more subtle than in my original draft, or at least Caroline told me he had had made the changes. I never had any intention to deceive him, go behind his back or put anything in the book that he didn't want. It's his book and I've tried since the beginning of a very difficult project to get it exactly the way he wanted it....I cannot explain why at this late date he elected to launch such a mean, insensitive and cruel attack on my family and me. Whatever his reasoning I have asked Joe Fox, Marlon's editor at Random House, to excise all the sentences on Page 559 that could be interpreted as alluding to Christian's problems. Why he didn't just simply ask me or Joe to cut the passage or cut it himself, I don't know, although I have some suspicions about the source of the venom in his telephone call: As you know, he and I were close friends until a few weeks ago, until I refused to support his proposal to renege on the contract he signed to deliver his autobiography to Random House and I told him I thought what he wanted me to do was immoral and dishonest. I won't go into the details of what he wanted me to do, but it raised issues of integrity that I couldn't live with.

At the time you told me he was distraught over my remarks. I suspect he has now decided that I am his enemy because I disagreed with him and wouldn't support a plan that, incidentally, I'm certain Random House would never have let him get away with. I could pass off his weird, irrational outburst as an indication that he's flipped his lid because of a passionate and understandable desire to protect his children, or I could speculate that he is unable to handle criticism or disagreement from someone he is fond of but cannot control. But when he threatened my family he passed over the line. My wife--whom you know--is terrified by what he said on the telephone and is afraid for the well being of our children. I want to emphasize to you, as Marlon's lawyer, that we take his threats at face value and seriously so, and that will do whatever is necessary to assure he does not carry them out. I would be grateful if you would acknowledge in a reply, as Marlon's lawyer, that you have received this notice and advise us that he has withdrawn his threats once he is assured that the sentences he wants removed from the manuscript have been cut. Now is the time to advise Joe Fox and Harry Evans of any further changes he wants to make.

An apology would also be appropriate, but that seems unlikely given Marlon's psyche...

I made sure the passage was cut from the galley proofs and Random House kept on its schedule to publish *Brando: Songs My Mother Taught Me* in October.

The summer passed silently between us. In early September one of Marlon's sisters, Jocelyn, called and said Marlon was depressed and remorseful over our estrangement. Would I be willing to hear his apology?

When he called he initially acted as if nothing had happened between us. I was as cold as I could be and asked him if he was going to apologize, and he asked me to forget what he'd said; it was a roundabout apology, but one I knew was difficult for him.

He said he wanted to resume our friendship, and we did.

When *Brando: Songs My Mother Taught Me* was published, nearly simultaneously in a dozen or so countries, a *New York Times* critic called the book "so weird it's wonderful," and it was soon rising on the paper's best seller list. A London paper described it as perhaps the best, most honest autobiography of an actor ever published. But along with raves were critics who didn't like it, many because of Marlon's refusal to write about his marriages or children.

Under his contract with Random House, Marlon had agreed to sit for at least one major television interview. Barbara Walters, Diane Sawyer and other TV journalists made a pitch for the interview but Marlon decided on CNN's Larry King, whom he knew from previous contacts.

The hour long interview on *Larry King Live* was a disaster for Marlon's image and book sales. When King arrived with his camera crew at Marlon's home, Marlon walked out of his bedroom shoeless, full of himself, not very likeable, constantly trying to one up and verbally fence with King.   He wanted to talk about anything except the book, including half baked ideas about the world's food shortages, making a fool of himself long before ending the interview by kissing King on the lips.

Panicked, the publicity staff at Random House tried to contain the losses by sending me on a hastily arranged book tour, but the damage had been done. Although sales were strong in many foreign countries, *Brando: Songs My Mother Taught Me* fell off the US best seller lists after a few weeks, and I don't think Random House made a profit on it.

46

Marlon accepted a small part in a movie with Johnny Depp set in Ireland, *Divine Rapture*, but his visit to Ireland was brief. Producers ran out of money two weeks after filming began, although they couldn't get back the $1 million they'd already paid Marlon, a non-refundable down payment on his $4 million contract, and he went home after two weeks a little richer.

Once Christian entered prison Marlon returned to the emotional devils tormenting Cheyenne At the psychiatric hospital in Tahiti, her depression and anxiety had worsened and doctors tentatively diagnosed her with schizophrenia. Twice, she tried unsuccessfully to commit suicide by swallowing sleeping pills.

Marlon wanted her brought to a clinic in the United States but French Polynesian judges refused to let her leave French jurisdiction because Dag Drollet's family had filed a suit accusing her of sharing liability for the murder of Drollet.

Marlon was also named in the suit. Because of it he never visited Tetiaroa again.

He arranged to have Cheyenne flown to Paris and met her there, where she was treated at first one psychiatric clinic, then another. Marlon called me in Carmel most days from Paris, reporting on his hopes for her improvement, usually reporting a lack of it, along with accounts of constant battles with French paparazzi.

After several weeks, Marlon flew home and Cheyenne, then 25, returned to Tahiti. A few weeks after her return, on April 16, 1995, she hanged herself in a bedroom at the home Marlon had bought for her family.

For almost a month, Marlon didn't return my phone calls. Later, he told me that as soon as he'd heard about Cheyenne's death he sent home his secretarial assistants, his maid and gardeners and locked himself inside the house.

Although I never observed Marlon as an affectionate or especially supportive father, he was nevertheless passionately protective of his children and emotionally vulnerable to their difficulties, especially the two tragedies of his later life--Christian's arrest and Cheyenne's death— and each sent him into long periods of depression.

He suffered even more not long after Cheyenne's death when *Tim*, his big mastiff and favorite dog (and my sometime bedmate in the guesthouse), died. Once more, he sent his staff home and said he wanted to be left alone in his bedroom and he remained there several days.

Marlon was furious when Petra, his adopted daughter for whom he'd obsessively spent almost a million dollars to make James Clavell acknowledge he was her biological father, made a documentary film about schizophrenia that focused in part on Cheyenne and the impact of the disease on patients' families.

"She's dead to me," he told me the evening he learned about the documentary.

After an Ivy League education, Petra had earned a law degree at the University of Southern California and decided to specialize in legal issues of mental health, largely, she said, because of Cheyenne, with whom she'd been close.

One critic called the film sensitive and sophisticated but it violated Marlon's rule against discussing the family publicly. Almost immediately, he rewrote his will, cutting her off with these words:

"All provisions of my will shall be interpreted as though Petra had predeceased me."

Petra's mother, Caroline Barrett, the Eurasian former mistress of Clavell who'd been Marlon's assistant for more than a decade, resigned and subsequently sued him after he tried to retrieve almost $200,00 that he claimed was a loan and she claimed was a gift to buy a home in London.

Christina Ruiz, the Guatemalan immigrant who'd started work as Marlon's house maid and became the mother of three of his children, was distraught because he'd refused repeatedly to marry her or even live together with her as man and wife. After he virtually banned her from his home except for visits by his children, she sued him for more than $100 million, claiming she required more than $10,000 a month alone for the children's schools (one child was autistic) as well as the cost of running the home Marlon had bought her complete with swimming pool and tennis court. (When he bought the home circa 1989 it cost about $500,000; after the real estate bubble of the nineties, its value was closer to $2 million.)

Financially, Marlon was falling behind, facing overdue taxes and annual expenses—"my nut"-- of more than $1 million; his real estate was mortgaged and re-mortgaged and he was living partly on proceeds from refinancing his property.

Reluctantly, he took small parts in several less than distinguished films including *Score*, with Robert DeNiro, *The Brave* directed by Johnny Depp, and *Free Money*, which was never released except as a DVD.

For all of his problems, Marlon kept insisting to me that he was going to become a billionaire.

The gold, he said, would now be mined from DVDs.

47

My telephone call to the executive at the Pennsylvania offices of QVC, the television retailing show, must have seemed odd: I identified myself as a former reporter who helped Marlon Brando write his memoirs, and said:

"I'm going to say something that will probably make you think I'm crazy, but I'm not making it up. Marlon Brando would like to speak to you about an idea he thinks you'll be interested in."

I offered him one of Marlon's unlisted phone numbers, one he ordinarily answered himself because it was reserved for calls from his children, and suggested someone from QVC call him to hear what he had to say. Marlon had become intensely interested in home shopping networks and Internet retailers because of their ability to move high volumes of merchandise in a short time, and he wanted to cash in on it using his status as a celebrity.

Once again he offered me ten per cent of our profits if I'd help him get the business started. I fell for it again, for awhile.

Marlon initially proposed pitching *Marlon Brando Conga Drums* on QVC--he'd been playing Afro-Cuban drums since his early days as a New York actor and had fashioned one of his own design—that he offered to demonstrate on the air. This project in time fell by the wayside, as did his proposal to sell electric eels over the air as a solution to generate electricity at remote locations such as his atoll in Tahiti. Finally, he settled on making a DVD about acting and selling it on the Internet. He figured the market was huge.

"Everybody's an actor, everybody lies, " he told me. Everyone conceals the truth sometime, he claimed, during romances and marriage; they lie at work, when they talk to their parents or kids, even their friends at church.

As an actor, he'd teach them how to lie more effectively.

Just as he did when he hatched his dream for *Tahiti Rain*, he picked up a calculator and began figuring our potential profits, calculating how much he thought we could make by selling his DVD; his estimates soon reached $100 million, multiplying thousands of sales at $20 per DVD, although I had to correct his math, reducing even his most optimistic estimate of our first year proceeds to $10 million.

QVC sent a woman to Marlon's home to discuss what he wanted to sell and in Carmel I eavesdropped on their conversation via Marlon's open cell phone.

The QVC executive was encouraging but surprised his product wasn't ready to sell. He said he was working on it and would get back to her shortly.

Thus began our efforts to produce *Lying for a Living*.

He rented a space in Los Angeles and invited more than a dozen actors to what he called a "master class" that, among other things, would demonstrate that even a person with no experience could be taught to act—and lie-- credibly.

Sean Penn, Robin Williams, Nick Nolte, Leonardo DeCaprio, Michael Jackson, Jon Voight and other stars responded to his invitation. Marlon hired Tony Kaye, a Brit, as director, but he quit after two days following an argument with Marlon because he'd shown up dressed as Osama Bin Laden and tried to teach Marlon had to teach his class.

Each day or two, Marlon's assistant, Angela Borlaza, a 32 year old Filipina woman who'd originally been hired as a maid and cook but was increasingly and effectively taking over the management of Marlon's life following Caroline Barrett's departure, sent me a video cassette recording of the latest filming, which I was to start editing into a coherent, saleable lesson-filled DVD.

A total of 16 tapes came in the mail, their arrival reminding me of Old Hollywood, when after each day's shooting producers watched the latest "rushes" or "dailies."

It didn't take long to realize this project was doomed, or at least my part in it.

On the first day of his master class Marlon walked on stage dressed as a woman wearing a blonde wig, lipstick and rouge and introduced the group to his first student, a homeless man he'd just met emptying an ashcan behind the theater. (I never knew why he chose to meet his first day students in drag.)

A day or two later, Marlon, wanting to do as little work himself as possible, asked some of his famous friends like Nolte and Penn to improvise a scene and explain their acting techniques to volunteers he'd recruited off the street. Except for a funny riff improvised by Robin Williams, none of it worked as acting lessons. Everyone seemed bewildered by what Marlon wanted them to do. Nolte bolted from the class, saying he couldn't figure how what was going on and didn't want to reveal his acting techniques to strangers.

"I think we need some professional people, Hollywood editors," I told Marlon, and that ended my role in the production of *Lying for a Living*.

48

For several years we had not spoken much about Michael Jackson, but I was soon to discover they had become close friends— like father and son, almost literally.

Marlon still telephoned at all hours to talk about whatever was on his mind, usually arcane topics that ranged from the future of nanotechnology to the "nature of evil." (He believed any culture could produce a Hitler because evil was an inherent and irreversible element of human nature, a product of atavistic DNA.). Some nights (until Sandy and I switched off the phones at 10 pm) he'd wake me late at night and want to muse about Shakespeare or recite a speech from *Hamlet*; once, apparently bored by whatever he'd been doing, he gave a perfectly nuanced recital of his "I could have been a contender" taxicab speech to Rod Steiger in *"On the Waterfront."* He reported on the progress of his latest diet, which changed with the seasons and over the years. Because of his weight, he'd been told that despite the potential value of his name on a marquee he was unlikely to get a job because producers couldn't't afford the required insurance on his life, so he caromed from one diet to the next—an all banana diet one week, the next a diet restricted to citrus and green vegetables or another, which lasted for months and seemed to have worked in reducing his weight, consisted only of lettuce dressed in lemon juice.

Although he was reluctant to acknowledge it, I think he was beginning to accept that his health was at risk because of his weight. I worried about the harm to his body by such a radical diet, although he boasted he'd already lost more than forty pounds.

I found myself fielding more and more calls from producers and others—photographer Richard Avedon and the *New Yorker* writer Lillian Ross, for example—who heard I was in touch with Marlon and asked me to arrange an audience with him or at least get him to return a phone call. As best as I recall, he never responded to any of the messages I passed on.

In the summer of 2001, Jackson asked Marlon to appear with him at a show in New York's Madison Square Garden in September celebrating his thirtieth year as an entertainer.

Marlon told me he initially turned him down, then said he'd do it for a million dollars.

"Michael's a good businessman, and first he said he couldn't afford it. But I knew he could, so I turned him down and said 'let me know' and he came up with the money."

As part of the million dollar deal, Jackson agreed to fly Marlon to New York in a corporate jet and persuaded him to make a brief appearance with him in a 13 minute video, *You Rock My World.*

Marlon's part in Jackson's Madison Square Garden show two days before the 9/11 attacks on the World Trade Center was a crazy disaster. After a bizarre entrance in which he was rolled on to the stage in an easy chair, he introduced himself:

"You may be thinking, 'who is that old fat fart sitting there?'"

He praised Jackson, then launched a wacky ten minute rant during which he removed his watch and said: "In the last minute, 100,000 children have been hacked to death with a machete."

The audience booed him off the stage, and his million-dollar appearance was cut from the subsequent TV production of Jackson's show.

49

Marlon had not given up on *Lying for a Living,* still certain it would make him a billionaire. But to get it launched he told me he needed to convince Jackson to invest in the project.

He and Jackson, he said, were going to produce a series of DVDs that would include not only acting lessons but footage of Marlon and Jackson interviewing each other on Marlon's atoll in Tahiti and Jackson had pledged to provide millions to finance the project.

A message left by Jackson on an answering machine played in court in an unrelated lawsuit involving a financial partner of Jackson indicated how interested Marlon had become in Jackson's money.

Jackson's voice is heard telling the financial partner that Marlon was pressing him hard for cash to finance what he called "the Marlon Brando Project."

"He's a wonderful man," Jackson said. "He's a god. He wants a lot of money. He wants to get things done right now."

In February, 2003, a British television journalist, Martin Bashir, after spending months trailing him with a camera crew, released a video called *Living with Michael Jackson* in which Jackson was seen holding hands with a twelve year old boy and admitting he often slept with young boys in the same bed, although he denied sexual contact with them.

"The most loving thing to do is to share your bed with someone," he said.

The interview, shown on television networks around the world, led to a hurricane of negative publicity for Jackson and eventually a renewed prosecution (and acquittal) on child abuse charges.

After Bashir's interview Marlon called and asked me to help him make a video to rebut the documentary.

I was to be introduced as a former *New York Times* correspondent and interview Jackson on camera, who'd present himself as misunderstood and innocent of abusing the children featured in Bashir's program.

I don't remember every word I said during the next few minutes, but I remember the first four words:

"Are you fucking crazy?"

Why would I do that? I asked him.

"Money."

"Fuck you."

I said we'd spent months if not years plotting to stop Jackson from molesting children and now he wanted me to help him cover it up?

I really exploded.

I reminded him of an affidavit signed by the child whom Jackson had paid almost $22 million. The affidavit described intimate, repeated sexual contacts—oral sex and mutual masturbation-- between the child and Jackson in Jackson's bed.

"Do you realize how much sexual abuse can affect a child for the rest of his life?

"What changed you? What's happened to you?"
His voice tightened, a tone I recognized when he felt he was on the defensive.

He said Jackson had suffered years of mistreatment, abuse and exploitation by a father who relentlessly demeaned and humiliated him, who beat him with a belt and locked him in a closet if he didn't perform at his best. Because of physical and mental abuse, he never had a chance to grow up like a normal child, Marlon said. He was over 40 years old, but he still thought of himself as a child.

He said he had "spiritually" adopted Jackson as his son, Jackson now called him "Dad" and he looked to him for fatherly guidance. He wanted Jackson to think of himself as Marlon's son.

Marlon said he had even set aside a half acre on Tetiaroa for Jackson to build a home and live as a Brando.

For Marlon, I realized later, hearing Jackson's claims about his father may have been like touching a live electrical wire: Jackson's story was in some ways an echo of his own life, a parallel history of a domineering father who humiliated a son too small to fight back. It was the theme of his life.

Still, I wondered:

As we argued, he claimed that he had offered to be Jackson's surrogate father because it was how he always responded when the powerful abused the weak. In fighting for the rights of Indians, blacks and impoverished untouchables in India, Marlon said he had done the same thing.

But I couldn't help remembering how often he mentioned he needed money and how large Jackson's fortune was and how he regarded Jackson as a kind of cash machine.

In the end, whatever his empathy might have been for Jackson or how deep his concern for the children, I suspect Marlon, in casting aside his initial concern for the boys who visited *Neverland*, and slept in Jackson's bed was ultimately in it for the money—Jackson's money.

The last time we talked about Michael Jackson, Marlon told me he had begun sleeping overnight with him in the same bed, his arms around him.

He didn't say whether there was sexual contact between them.

He didn't say, and I didn't ask.

50

On April 3. 2004, Angela arranged an 80th birthday party for
Marlon for about ten friends at his home on Mulholland Drive.
Among them were Harry Dean Stanton, an actor friend; movie
producer Mike Medavoy, a handful of others.

After Angela served a buffet of Filipino specialties Marlon
walked slowly into the living room where he and I had spent so many
hours. He looked tired and thinner than I'd ever seen him. He was
pulling an oxygen tank behind him that was connected to a plastic pipe
fixed in his nostrils. I hadn't seen him in months and was surprised by
his slow steps.

Stanton had brought a guitar and played a couple of songs and
Marlon and I exchanged a few words but he said he was tired and left
after about twenty minutes. I went to his bedroom and said goodbye
to him at his bedside.

Sandy and I spent the night in the guest house where I'd always
stayed before. In the morning Angela cooked us breakfast and said
Marlon was anxious to talk to me. He was still asleep, but wanted us
to stick around so we could talk when he woke up.

I was anxious to get home and knew from experience we might
have to wait hours for him to get out of bed, so I told Angela we had
to leave for home and we left, a decision I regret.

After the party, Marlon and I talked by phone most days. I remember once telling him: "Don't you die on me."

"I'm trying not to," he said.

About three months after his birthday party, on July 1, Sandy and I arrived home after visiting relatives in Sacramento. The red light on my answering machine was blinking with two messages:

The first, logged at 2:15 pm, was from Marlon.

"Bob, you there?

Silence.

Marlon must have been waiting for me to pick up the phone if I was there.

About fifteen more seconds passed....

"Bob, call me when you can," he said and hung up.

The second message, about six hours later, was from Angela's sister, Vie, a nurse:

"I'm sorry to have to tell you that Mr. Brando passed away tonight at 6:20."
He died of pulmonary fibrosis, a lung disease he'd been fighting for more than a year.

A few weeks later, I delivered a eulogy at a memorial service for Marlon at Medavoy's home in Beverly Hills.

I'd typed out a few words, expecting to have a lectern where I could place my notes and read from them, but there was just a microphone, so I had to hold the sheets of paper in my hands.

As I reached the microphone, I looked out at some of the most recognizable faces on the planet.

The first person I saw was Michael Jackson sitting in the front row about four feet from me, his face a curious white mask looking up at me.

Sitting near him were Barbra Streisand, Jack Nicholson, Sean Penn, John Travolta, Warren Beatty and just about every front rank star in the Hollywood constellation---more than 150 people, mostly actors, honoring the man often called the world's greatest actor.

"In 1988," I began, "Marlon called me from out of the blue and asked me to help him write a book, which in time became his autobiography. Since then we've spoken almost every day about something...I know most people will remember him for the roles he played...Stanley Kowalski, Terry Malloy, Col. Kurtz and others... but for me he was just somebody to hang out with, a friend."

I mentioned a time Sandy was in the hospital briefly and Marlon sent her flowers and a note signed by Marlon's mastiff, *Tim*, with *Tim's* huge paw print inscribed from an ink pad.

"*Tim* also died not long ago, and in many ways the two of them were alike: Both were big; both could be intimidating and both were *vulnerable*...."

I told them the history of *Marlon Brando's Tahiti Rain*, "revealed here for the first time...

"We got somebody from Canada to put up a million dollars, but it was ultimately a failure," I said, "but what do you expect from a business started by an actor and a writer?," bringing laughter from the audience of actors.

By then, I was choking back tears, couldn't continue and sat down.

Early the next day, when Sandy and I were back home in Carmel, Angela called and said she was in a car with Miko headed for *Neverland*.

Michael Jackson, she said, had been moved by my eulogy and wanted Sandy and me to come to *Neverland*.

I told her, no, I didn't want to visit *Neverland*.

Afterword

My daughter, Susan, was first to suggest this book. My thanks to her and to my son, Steve, for their help in putting it together. When I have used direct quotations, I have done my best to recall the exact words spoken during the many conversations reported in the memoir, while acknowledging that memories can be fallible. To augment my memories I also relied on notes made at the time, reminiscences of friends and family members, interviews, tape recordings, letters and other documents and the archives of *The New York Times* .

Thanks also, for various gestures along the way, to Jonathan Coleman, Sister Anne Louise, W.A. Kamrath, Jackson Turner Main, Jeanie Wakeland-Von Bargen, John Howe, Oscar Liden, Dick Witkin, Ted Bolwell, Sharon Johnson, Bruce Webster, Punch Sulzberger, A.M. Rosenthal, David R. Jones, Edward Klein, Arthur Gelb, Michael George, Alice Mayhew, Aaron Levy, Angela Borlaza, Mike Jensen and George Diskant.

Finally, my thanks and my love to Sandy, who put up with my quirks and helped make each day a celebration.

What could be more fun than being a reporter?

Or marrying your dream girl at 21 and embarking on a thrilling partnership for life, sharing it with two kind and compassionate children and their inspiring offspring?

With a notebook and a great deal of curiosity, I traveled the world, top to bottom, from the Arctic Circle to the South Pole.

I hung out with murderers, spies, a President, mobsters, generals, movie stars and scientists who helped shape our future.

I watched history unfold and wrote about it.

Not only was my journey free, I got paid for it. (I would have done it for nothing.)

Not bad for the kid from the trailer camp at the corner of Prairie Avenue and Century Boulevard.

About the Author

Robert Lindsey, former Chief West Coast Correspondent of *The New York Times,* is author of *The Falcon and the Snowman* and other bestselling books and a recipient of the Gold Dagger and Edgar Allen Poe awards. He is married and lives in California.

9 781481 201193